The Art of Bookmaking

Other titles by this author from High Stakes

Nursery Class
The 2006 World Cup Betting Guide
The Tote Placepot Annual NH 03/04
Win at Fixed Odds Football Betting

The Art of Bookmaking

And the Compiling of Odds

Malcolm Boyle

High Stakes

First published in 2006 by High Stakes Publishing,
21 Great Ormond Street, London WC1N 3JB
www.highstakespublishing.com

© Malcolm Boyle 2006

A CIP catalogue record for this book is available from the British Library.

ISBN 10: 1 84344 026 1
EAN 13: 978 1 84344 026 0

2 4 6 8 10 9 7 5 3 1

Typeset by Windrush Publishing Services, Gloucestershire
Printed and bound in Great Britain by Cox & Wyman, Reading.

To Wendy

Horse racing (gambling in general) dominates a great deal of what otherwise might be classed as leisure time, and the partners in our lives have to be extremely tolerant of the situation. I picked a great one out of the 'paddock' in all honesty, and my wife has been my personal favourite ever since. We've managed to foal a couple of corkers in Charlie and Lucy, even though my stud fee now sits at an all time low.

I thank God for what I have, and Wendy who has delivered the rest.

Contents

Foreword

Having read through the pre-edited chapters, I confess that I'm not at all sure if I have written this book on behalf of the bookmakers or the punters!

I offer advice to bookmakers to take advantage of punters on one hand, but berate the layers on occasions because of the lack of invention to fight off the opposition of betting exchanges. Bookmakers have had their own way for far too long, and only the strong will survive the exchanges.

I am heartened by the fact that Freddie Williams (no less) was literally the first person to enquire about the book, and no, he was not potentially looking to criticise the publication, according to his daughter Julie. It is this type of attitude that will win the day, because as big a player as the Williams' team is in the ring, it is not afraid of learning more in its quest to offset modern technology. I also like to think that the Williams' team have their ears open to new ideas, which I think I can offer, certainly as far as new wagers are concerned.

Part of this publication is also written to offer punters the chance to level the playing field, by acquiring knowledge to form their own prices before placing a wager.

Essentially, every punter should know the minimum price

they are prepared to accept before placing a bet. This book will hopefully point the punters (and the bookmakers) in the right direction.

CHAPTER 1

Basics of Odds Compiling
and Legalities

Without wishing to get dragged into legal jargon, I could not write this book without mentioning the legal requirements of what we class as an old-fashioned bookmaker, which is as far removed to those of you who are looking to become unofficial, but not illegal, layers on the betting exchanges.

The simple truth comes in two parts.

You are legally required as a person to apply for a bookmaker's permit. This is not to be confused with a bookmaker's licence, which actually applies to a place of business (betting shop), which requires a licence with which to trade. A person requires a permit to be classed as a bookmaker which, given other financial criteria (references), would allow them to set up as a layer on-course. They would then require a licence for any premises that might be bought or leased to be utilised as a betting shop. Both the permit, for a person and a licence, for premises, can only be obtained through a court hearing.

Permits are easier to obtain because, providing there is no history of problems relating to the person who is applying for the permit, there is no obvious reason for the court to deny the application.

Licensed premises are entirely another matter.

There could be umpteen reasons why a magistrate might be convinced that the local area does not require more premises where people can legally bet though, equally, it is far easier to convince local people of the requirement of such outlets these days.

Since the national lottery came into being in 1994, local magistrates have, in a fashion, had their hands tied, as post offices, newsagents and any local leaseholder can seemingly encourage people to part with their money through televised bingo.

Potential bookmakers have jumped on the bandwagon and applications for licences are supposedly backed up by disabled persons who cannot gain access to the betting shop down the road because of the lack of a ramp or suitable toilet facilities.

The magistrates have about as much chance of denying an application nowadays as Foinavon had of winning the Grand National in 1967!

Now we have got the legal jargon out of the way, we can approach the subject in question, which is bookmaking, in concise, yet as easy to read detail as I can offer.

I was a mere lad of thirteen when the aforementioned Foinavon won the Grand National but had already backed my first winner of the great race in Team Spirit three years earlier and was well on the way to being hooked by the sport of kings. It would take half the book to establish my experience within the business, suffice to say that this is my sixth published title, following efforts as a betting shop manager, an odds compiler, a bookmaker (both on and off course), a commentator, a greyhound steward, a statistician for both Tote Direct and Channel 4 Racing and a daily columnist for sportinglife.com.

These points are not made to boast in any form because, like most of us within the trade, I haven't perfected anything. The facts are simply listed in the hope that the reader will understand that I have been around the block a few times and that I am still running!

Bookmakers or turf accountants, to offer such professionals the correct term, officially opened their betting shops for business back in May 1961, though 'runners' were still to be found on many a street corner in those days, with selections scribbled on the back of cigarette packets and scraps of paper. William Hill was arguably the first of the bookmakers to hit the big time and I remember visiting their head office at Hill House over Blackfriars Bridge in London back in 1970. Men stood on ladders literally chalking up prices on massive blackboards at Hill House, though companies producing whiteboards and marker pens were soon to flourish through the logical requirement of betting shops, which simply did not have the space to accommodate the old fashioned ways.

Punters used to watch the list of runners and prices every bit as much as they focus on the screens nowadays. It was as though they could visualise the race by staring at the list of runners on what can only be described as sheets of discarded wallpaper, which was conveniently cut down to size to accommodate the number of runners in any given race.

The growth of the industry after many years of trading has been immense and punters have never had it so good, to quote a famous politician. Unfashionable problems still grace the sport of course, such as a couple of areas of frost that suspend play for an entire afternoon.

It beggars belief that areas the size of football pitches

can be declared playable in the dead of night, yet race meetings can be abandoned due to the total lack of effort of the powers that be, not the staff, at a horse race venue. As long as the insurance is in place, why worry about folk such as trainers, jockeys and punters, who really keep the sport alive and who have to travel hundreds of miles to reach their destination. It's much easier for a steward, dare I say a clerk of the course, to suggest that we 'really must abandon' when not enough effort has been put into place to protect the meeting initially. Rays of sunshine can pour down for hours on a strip of land that has been neglected, with the meetings written off hours earlier, despite the fact that the British horse racing industry is one of the largest employers in Europe.

I digress...

Another politician (aside from Harold Macmillan), the late Robin Cook, befriended the sport of horse racing to the extent that his name will be remembered through an important race on Cheltenham's impressive calendar and there should not be a punter in the country that can argue with that decision. Aside from being a friend of John McCririck, Robin made every move a winning one on behalf of the industry, not least of which was his work to rid the sport of betting tax.

Several politicians have enjoyed horse racing from a leisure perspective and I remember a few of them making reference to my first book *How To Win at the Tote Placepot*. The late Woodrow Wyatt (Chairman of the Tote) had asked for the book to be placed as a gift on tables for guests at the official Tote luncheon, which was held a few days before the start of the Cheltenham Festival.

The guest speaker – the then Chancellor of the

Exchequer, Kenneth Clarke as I recall - made reference to the publication in his speech, suggesting that he was a regular player of the said wager.

Her Majesty, the late Queen Mother, gave royal approval to the sport of kings, so I guess that politicians were comfortable talking about a sport disparaged by those that did not look beyond the scruffy image of the business during its early years.

Bookmaking is not an exact science as you might appreciate and whilst I will concentrate on sport in this publication, betting on general elections since the war might best explain the potential problem when laying prices to the public.

Since a coalition was in power in 1918, 22 general elections (at the time of writing) have been contested by just the main two parties, as far as a realistic chance of winning is concerned. Bookmakers however, have priced up the other parties simply because they are obliged to do so by definition.

As an example, the layers could not merely offer 4/9 Labour and 13/8 the Conservatives, because there is a third party (at the very least) to consider. Bookmakers must offer odds when there is even the slightest chance that a winning scenario is alive; hence likely betting in the example quoted would be 1/2 Labour, 7/4 the Conservatives and 80/1 the Liberal Democrats, even though the third party has rarely, if ever, been close to winning a general election.

An old adage still exists (if only in principle) from a punter's perspective, that if a player cannot win, they cannot lose. Basically, the punter MUST be offered the chance to win, or bets could be deemed null and void, in theory at least. The Liberals must therefore be featured in the betting, if only to satisfy the potential demand.

I was at a greyhound meeting recently, dining out with a group of friends when the following scenario came into play. One of the punters had wagered a place only bet on trap one and the greyhound duly obliged by finishing in the first two in a six-dog event.

The lady in question seemed perfectly happy with her returned stake, which was exactly the same as she had played, two pounds in this instance, which raises the question, should all stakes on that race have been refunded to losing punters, as a scenario took place where, because of the way punters had gambled on the local tote, no winnings were accrued by people who had invested correctly on this particular greyhound?

If the punters in question could not win, that is receive extra money along with their stake, why should they risk the investment being lost initially? This scenario occurred because there simply was not enough money in the tote pool to pay winners out, over and above the stake that the punters had invested on a specific trap.

The point I am making is, how many other greyhounds that lost that evening would not have won money (over and above the stake) for their investors, because of the imperfections of the tote pools at the meeting?

In the strictest sense, monies should have been returned to punters who stood no chance of winning before the traps had opened on the relevant events. By definition, in contrast to the greyhound example, betting shops cannot offer odds on an event where they leave a potential winner out of the equation.

In the case of the general election that I offered as an example, all parties that stand for the election in question would be quoted in the betting, if only on application perhaps, provided a party had enough representatives standing at local elections whereby they could form a government if the result went their way. This is why bookmakers are obliged to quote a price for the Liberal Democrats, at this moment in time, as the party is a genuine contender to form a government as far as betting is concerned, irrespective of the eventual result.

Journalists that report on general elections are not obvious punters, unlike those who offer opinions about horse racing. Indeed, journalists that steer clear of gambling are as rare as Birmingham City captains lifting trophies in the football world! Racing journalists do not always understand the logistics of betting however, as was the case after the Bula Hurdle at Cheltenham back in November 2005.

The 'journo' in question was obviously not impressed by the performance of the winner Harchibald and berated bookmakers for reducing the price to around the 4/1 mark for Noel Meade's raider to win the Champion Hurdle, which was due to be contested four months later.

The first point to make is that Rooster Booster is the only winner of the 'Bula' in recent seasons to go on and win the Champion Hurdle during the same campaign. Whilst bookmakers would often consider such a statistic when assessing prices for the March showdown, the layers ignored the scenario for a very good reason, which the journalist in question blatantly failed to appreciate. The logic about each way betting was lost on the reporter, because with bookmakers offering a quarter of the odds a place (1-2-3), any odds higher than 4-1 would have created a bet to nothing from an each way perspective.

A bet to nothing, for those that are not familiar with the term, is a wager that a punter will place which, supposedly, will guarantee their stake being returned if the relevant selection is only placed in the contest in question. If the selection went on to actually win the race, so much the better from the punter's perspective. There is no such thing as a guaranteed return of course but there most certainly are merchants hovering around bookmaking outlets waiting for mistakes to be made on the betting front.

Bookmakers will happily cater for a potential return of stake to the punter, given that the layers would be holding on to clients' investments for a period of three months or more, if investors had wanted to back a horse (such as Harchibald) to win the Champion Hurdle in November. As accountants first and foremost, they will appreciate that money is better in their keeping than the opposite scenario. If Harchibald (in this instance) ran into place money, the layers would simply shrug their shoulders, happy in the knowledge that they could have cleaned up by securing all the investment. By offering 9/2 or more however, the layers would have been offering punters the edge from an each way perspective. Odds of 9/8 a place are not particularly attractive to potential investors but that is not the point.

The word accountant is the operative word in this case, as offering a punter any edge is against the layers better nature, especially when the horse in question is Harchibald. Win, lose or draw, Harchibald would, if previous races are anything to go by, be the only horse in the field that is guaranteed to be cantering coming to the final flight at Cheltenham. Whether the gelding actually went on to win the Champion Hurdle is not the point.

I have decided not to edit this piece of text in the event

of Harchibald's defeat in the Christmas Hurdle and subsequent injury at Leopardstown next time out. The going was very much against Noel Meade's raider and the trainer was seriously considering withdrawing the horse up to three quarters of an hour before flag-fall. Paul Carberry rode another of his less than perfect rides, allowing Brave Inca a lead that he was never going to peg back on the gluey going, especially with Tony McCoy aboard the winner.

Some layers took the opinion that the horse was now worth laying from an each way perspective by quoting Harchibald at 5/1. I still believe this to be the wrong price. If Harchibald had been fit and racing on decent ground, Noel Meade's Perugino gelding would have been in the thick of things, of that I have no doubt. Thanks to the injury that kept Harchibald out of the Champion Hurdle, we will never know if 5/1 was the correct price.

Odds compilers are judged on whether they have offered the correct prices before an event, irrespective of the eventual result.

At the time of writing, the layers that accommodated Harchibald are smiling. If they make repeated mistakes however, the smiles will be wiped off their respective faces. Odds compilers are only as good as their last results and so are bookmakers. The difference is that odds compilers will learn by experience, naïve bookmakers will trust to luck and luck does not last. The Art of Bookmaking is making the right decision, irrespective of the eventual result.

I was attending my final interview for a vacant odds compiler position with one of the major bookmakers, when I was asked a final, fictitious question.

Given that all three athletes came into the race on their best form, I was asked how I would price up a race over a mile at Crystal Palace (in perfect conditions) between Steve Ovett, Sebastian Coe and Steve Cram?

As quick as a flash, I quoted odds of 3/1 on both Steve Cram and Steve Ovett without any further comment. All was quiet for a few seconds before a bright spark commented, 'What type of answer is that?'

The chap in question was, fortunately, shot down in flames when the boss man accepted my explanation that Coe should not be laid if possible, because he was the only athlete of the three that would die for the cause, in my considered opinion. The rest of the panel was not consulted before the main man simply added, 'It's the type of answer that just won him the job!'

I soon learned that whatever prices I offered on behalf of the company they had to be backed up by facts and informed opinion, whereby my position within the company would not be called into question. Just one mistake with no back up would have seen me on my way.

Too many experts in this business rely on the form book, in my opinion, taking the 'relevant pounds for lengths beaten' between two horses too literally. If horse 'A' beats horse 'B' by a length at Ayr on good going over seven furlongs, in a similarly made up race that is not affected by the draw, horse 'B' might well reverse the form on four pounds better terms but only if the exact same scenario is in place for the re-match. That is my interpretation anyway. Should the second race be contested at Sandown's - right-handed track against Ayr's left-handed circuit, the original placings might well be reversed. The going should always be taken into account which could have another bearing on the outcome, whilst some horses give their best in small fields and others in competitive events, even before we take the draw into consideration. The relevant trainers of the two horses concerned might have endured a hot or cold run of form, whilst the availability of jockeys also enters the equation. All these factors must be taken into account before an odds compiler puts pen to paper; hence the job is nowhere near as simple as some experts might believe. Journalists are sometimes too busy in the bar to look at form and ante-post odds logically.

CHAPTER 2

Percentages

Everything in bookmaking literally revolves around percentages and a bookmaker has no chance whatsoever of surviving in the business if they cannot comprehend the figures involved. In truth, there is no requirement to be a professor of mathematics, just as long as you can handle mental arithmetic to a decent standard. Failing that, a good memory is essential.

The mistake that so many punters make, is that investors allow bookmakers to dictate the terms of betting yet, with a little application, the general public can become as informed as the market makers. Bookmakers are turf accountants by definition and like any other accountant, they need to balance their books. Turf accountants use percentages to dictate their transactions and there is no reason why you cannot become as mathematical in your approach to the betting war between bookmaker and punter.

The full percentage table is as follows:

Odds On%	Price	Odds Against%
50.0	EVS	50.0
52.4	11/10	47.6
54.5	6/5	45.5
55.6	5/4	44.4
57.9	11/8	42.1
60.0	6/4	40.0
61.9	13/8	38.1
63.6	7/4	36.4
65.2	15/8	34.8
66.7	2/1	33.3
69.2	9/4	30.8
71.4	5/2	28.6
73.3	11/4	26.7
75.0	3/1	25.0
76.9	10/3	23.1
77.8	7/2	22.2
80.0	4/1	20.0
81.8	9/2	18.2
83.3	5/1	16.7
84.6	11/2	15.4
85.7	6/1	14.3
86.7	13/2	13.3
87.5	7/1	12.5
88.3	15/2	11.7
88.9	8/1	11.1
89.5	17/2	10.5
90.0	9/1	10.0
90.9	10/1	9.1
91.7	11/1	8.3
92.3	12/1	7.7
93.3	14/1	6.7
94.1	16/1	5.9
94.7	18/1	5.3
95.2	20/1	4.8
95.8	22/1	4.2

Odds On%	Price	Odds Against%
96.2	25/1	3.8
96.6	28/1	3.4
97.0	33/1	3.0
97.6	40/1	2.4
98.0	50/1	2.0
98.5	66/1	1.5
98.8	80/1	1.2
99.0	100/1	1.0

You will quickly deduce that by adding the odds on figure to the odds against percentage for each price, the result is 100%, which is as it should be. Next time you see a horse backed from 25/1 to 12/1 (a difference of 3.9%) in a race do not be alarmed. Now you are in full possession of the facts, you will quickly deduce that the comparison is roughly the same as a favourite being backed into 15/8 from 9/4 (a difference of 4.0%), which is exactly why you need to digest these figures.

If you didn't know before, you will now recognise that a potential runner at 8/1 for any race represents 11.1% of the market from the bookmaker's perspective. Try to learn these figures parrot fashion if you can, or preferably, take a copy of these percentages with you when you wage war with the enemy, whether in a betting shop, on the Internet, or on the racecourse. Alternatively, you should be able to remember the figures if you round up/down the percentages to whole numbers, which will give you approximate details that are good enough to arm you with an important weapon against the bookmaker.

73.3% for example (4/11) would be rounded down to 73, whereas 26.7% (11/4 against) could be rounded up to 27.

You will be able to decide whether to back your judgement immediately when prices become available, having decided the odds that you are willing to accept before knowing the price that has been quoted. Using this method, you are the one who is dictating the betting scenario, not the bookmaker. The two basic terms when offering odds are over round and over broke, which basically tells you as a bookmaker if you are potentially (depending how punters react to the odds on offer) going to win or lose money in any given event.

Over round is the preferable scenario, as you (the layer) are compiling a book which suggests that the bookmaker is guaranteed to make a profit, from an accountant's perspective at least. By betting over round, the odds you are laying equal a 'book' of over 100%, hence if all the horses, in a racing scenario, are backed to win one hundred pounds, for example, you, the bookmaker, will be guaranteed a profit. The term 'book' constitutes all the odds on offer being added together using the percentage figures they represent.

If the odds for a six horse race are returned at 5/4 − 4/1 − 6/1 − 8/1 − 10/1 − 14/1, the potential profit for the bookmaker is 5.6% (from percentages of 44.4% − 20.0 − 14.3 − 11.1 − 9.1 − 6.7).

I wonder if you can spot the potential danger in the over round example?

As suggested in the opening chapter, a bookmaker offering 4/1 for the second favourite is in danger of laying a bet to nothing from the punter's perspective. The place terms for a six horse race offers potential punters the opportunity of backing horses at 4/1 (or more) chance of winning a bet, with the bonus of receiving their full stake back (or more) if the selection finishes second.

The bookmaker in this instance, would be best advised to bet 7/2 the second favourite, perhaps offering the outsiders at extended odds until the early prices have settled down. Conversely, in offering an over broke scenario, a bookmaker would potentially lose given the following example.

If the same six-runner race was priced up at 13/8 – 7/2 – 13/2 – 9/1 – 12/1 – 16/1, the potential loss for the bookmaker (in a perfect world of laying all horses to the same return) would be 2.8%, from percentages of 38.1% – 22.2 – 13.3 – 10.0 – 7.7 – 5.9, which add up to 97.2%.

The bookmaker in this over broke instance has protected their bet to nothing scenario about the second favourite but has been too generous with the rest of the prices.

Dutching is the punting term when investors are looking to back two or more horses (two or more more wagers given any betting scenario) in the same race or event. As a bookmaker, you should always be looking at the race from two viewpoints, both a layer's and a punter's perspective. Aside from a small player or Silver Ring punter, a bookmaker should always question why an investor has gambled on two (or more) selections. Is the punter in question merely indecisive, or have they seen an edge in the odds on offer?

Adding percentages together, you will find that the following prices of two betting scenarios added together equal the prices as follows:

2/1 & 2/1 = 1/2

2/1 & 9/4 = 4/7

2/1 & 5/2 = 8/13

2/1 & 11/4 = 4/6

2/1 & 3/1 = 8/11

2/1 & 7/2 = 4/5

2/1 & 4/1 = 10/11

2/1 & 9/2 = 20/21

2/1 & 5/1 = Evs

2/1 & 11/2 = 21/20

2/1 & 6/1 = 11/10

2/1 & 7/1 = 6/5

2/1 & 8/1 = 5/4

2/1 & 10/1 = 11/8

2/1 & 14/1 = 6/4

2/1 & 20/1 = 13/8

2/1 & 33/1 = 7/4

2/1 & 80/1 = 15/8

9/4 & 9/4 = 8/13

9/4 & 5/2 = 4/6

9/4 & 11/4 = 8/11

9/4 & 3/1 = 4/5

9/4 & 7/2 = 10/11

9/4 & 4/1 = Evs

9/4 & 9/2 = 21/20

9/4 & 5/1 = 11/10

9/4 & 6/1 = 6/5

9/4 & 13/2 = 5/4

9/4 & 15/2 = 11/8

9/4 & 10/1 = 6/4

9/4 & 12/1 = 13/8

9/4 & 18/1 = 7/4

9/4 & 25/1 = 15/8

9/4 & 33/1 = 2/1

9/4 & 80/1 = 85/40

5/2 & 5/2 = 8/11

5/2 & 11/4 = 4/5

5/2 & 10/3 = 10/11

5/2 & 7/2 = Evs

5/2 & 4/1 = 11/10

5/2 & 5/1 = 6/5

5/2 & 11/2 = 5/4

5/2 & 13/2 = 11/8

5/2 & 17/2 = 6/4

5/2 & 10/1 = 13/8

5/2 & 12/1 = 7/4

5/2 & 16/1 = 15/8

5/2 & 20/1 = 2/1

5/2 & 25/1 = 85/40

5/2 & 40/1 = 9/4

11/4 & 10/3 = Evs

11/4 & 7/2 = 21/20

11/4 & 9/2 = 5/4

11/4 & 11/2 = 11/8

11/4 & 13/2 = 6/4

11/4 & 15/2 = 13/8

11/4 & 9/1 = 7/4

11/4 & 12/1 = 15/8

11/4 & 14/1 = 2/1

11/4 & 16/1 = 85/40

11/4 & 25/1 = 9/4

11/4 & 40/1 = 5/2

3/1 & 3/1 = Evs

3/1 & 7/2 = 11/10

3/1 & 4/1 = 6/5

3/1 & 5/1 = 11/8

3/1 & 11/2 = 6/4   3/1 & 13/2 = 13/8
3/1 & 15/2 = 7/4   3/1 & 9/1 = 15/8
3/1 & 14/1 = 85/40   3/1 & 16/1 = 9/4
3/1 & 25/1 = 5/2   3/1 & 66/1 = 11/4

10/3 & 7/2 = 6/5   10/3 & 5/1 = 6/4
10/3 & 11/2 = 13/8   10/3 & 13/2 = 7/4
10/3 & 15/2 = 15/8   10/3 & 9/1 = 2/1
10/3 & 10/1 = 85/40   10/3 & 12/1 = 9/4
10/3 & 14/1 = 5/2   10/3 & 18/1 = 11/4
10/3 & 50/1 = 3/1

7/2 & 7/2 = 5/4   7/2 & 4/1 = 11/8
7/2 & 9/2 = 6/4   7/2 & 5/1 = 13/8
7/2 & 6/1 = 7/4   7/2 & 7/1 = 15/8
7/2 & 8/1 = 2/1   7/2 & 9/1 = 85/40
7/2 &11/1 = 9/4   7/2 &14/1 = 5/2
7/2 & 22/1 = 11/4   7/2 & 40/1 = 3/1
7/2 & 100/1 = 10/3

4/1 & 4/1 = 6/4   4/1 & 9/2 = 13/8
4/1 & 5/1 = 7/4   4/1 & 13/2 = 15/8
4/1 & 7/1 = 85/40   4/1 & 8/1 = 9/4
4/1 & 9/1 = 5/2   4/1 & 14/1 = 11/4
4/1 & 18/1 = 3/1   4/1 & 28/1 = 10/3
4/1 & 50/1 = 7/2

9/2 & 9/2 = 7/4   9/2 & 5/1 = 15/8
9/2 & 11/2 = 2/1   9/2 & 7/1 = 9/4
9/2 & 17/2 = 5/2   9/2 & 11/1 = 11/4
9/2 & 14/1 = 3/1   9/2 & 20/1 = 10/3
9/2 & 25/1 = 7/2   9/2 & 50/1 = 4/1

5/1 & 5/1 = 2/1   5/1 & 11/2 = 85/40
5/1 & 6/1 = 9/4   5/1 & 15/2 = 5/2
5/1 & 9/1 = 11/4   5/1 & 11/1 = 3/1
5/1 & 14/1 = 10/3   5/1 & 18/1 = 7/2
5/1 & 28/1 = 4/1   5/1 & 66/1 = 9/2

11/2 & 11/2 = 9/4   11/2 & 13/2 = 5/2
11/2 & 8/1 = 11/4   11/2 & 9/1 = 3/1
11/2 & 12/1 = 10/3   11/2 & 14/1 = 7/2
11/2 & 20/1 = 4/1   11/2 & 33/1 = 9/2
11/2 & 66/1 = 5/1

6/1 & 6/1 = 5/2   6/1 & 7/1 = 11/4
6/1 & 17/2 = 3/1   6/1 & 10/1 = 10/3
6/1 & 12/1 = 7/2   6/1 & 16/1 = 4/1
6/1 & 25/1 = 9/2   6/1 & 80/1 = 11/2

13/2 & 13/2 = 11/4   13/2 & 15/2 = 3/1
13/2 & 9/1 = 10/3   13/2 & 14/1 = 4/1
13/2 & 20/1 = 9/2   13/2 & 28/1 = 5/1
13/2 & 80/1 = 11/2   13/2 & 100/1 = 6/1

7/1 & 7/1 = 3/1   7/1 & 17/2 = 10/3
7/1 & 9/1 = 7/2   7/1 & 12/1 = 4/1
7/1 & 16/1 = 9/2   7/1 & 22/1 = 5/1
7/1 & 33/1 – 11/2   7/1 & 50/1 = 6/1
7/1 & 100/1 = 13/2

15/2 & 15/2 = 10/3   15/2 & 17/2 = 7/2
15/2 & 11/1 = 4/1   15/2 & 14/1 = 9/2
15/2 & 20/1 = 5/1   15/2 & 25/1 = 11/2
15/2 & 33/1 = 6/1   15/2 & 40/1 = 13/2
15/2 & 125/1 = 7/1

8/1 & 8/1 = 7/2   8/1 & 10/1 = 4/1
8/1 & 14/1 = 9/2   8/1 & 18/1 = 5/1
8/1 & 22/1 = 11/2   8/1 & 33/1 = 6/1
8/1 & 40/1 = 13/2   8/1 & 66/1 = 7/1
8/1 & 150/1 = 15/2

9/1 & 9/1 = 4/1   9/1 & 11/1 = 9/2
9/1 & 14/1 = 5/1   9/1 & 18/1 = 11/2
9/1 & 22/1 = 6/1   9/1 & 28/1 = 13/2
9/1 & 40/1 = 7/1   9/1 & 66/1 = 15/2
9/1 & 10/1 = 8/1

10/1 & 10/1 = 9/2	10/1 & 12/1 = 5/1
10/1 & 14/1 = 11/2	10/1 & 18/1 = 6/1
10/1 & 22/1 = 13/2	10/1 & 28/1 = 7/1
10/1 & 40/1 = 15/2	10/1 & 50/1 = 8/1
12/1 & 12/1 = 11/2	12/1 & 14/1 = 6/1
12/1 & 20/1 = 7/1	12/1 & 28/1 = 8/1
12/1 & 40/1 = 9/1	12/1 & 66/1 = 10/1
14/1 & 14/1 = 13/2	14/1 & 16/1 = 7/1
14/1 & 22/1 = 8/1	14/1 & 28/1 = 9/1
14/1 & 40/1 = 10/1	14/1 & 100/1 = 12/1
16/1 & 16/1 = 15/2	16/1 & 18/1 = 8/1
16/1 & 22/1 = 9/1	16/1 & 28/1 = 10/1
16/1 & 40/1 = 11/1	

Now you are aware of the percentages, evaluate any others yourself!

I should attempt to explain the perfect book for layers at this stage, offering an example of a six horse or dog race that, in a perfect world, would offer bookmakers unlimited cigars for the rest of their days.

In a typical betting scenario of making a 110.4 % book, prices might be offered like this:

Trap/horse number 1: 7/2 (22.2%)
Trap/horse number 2: 12/1 (7.7%)
Trap/horse number 3: 7/4 (36.4%)
Trap/horse number 4: 33/1 (3.0%)
Trap/horse number 5: 5/2 (28.6%)
Trap/horse number 6: 7/1 (12.5%)

Ideally, the greyhounds or horses would be backed accordingly, which would ensure a profit for the layers given any result:

£22 @ 7/2 equates to a return to the potential client of £99
£8 @ 12/1 equates to a return to the potential client of £104
£36 @ 7/4 equates to a return to the potential client of £99
£3 @ 33/1 equates to a return to the potential client of £102
£30 @ 5/2 equates to a return to the potential client of £105
£13 @ 7/1 equates to a return to the potential client of £104

The total invested is £112 in this example offering a maximum percentage profit of 11.6%, with a minimum haul of 6.2%.

Profit if trap/horse number 1 wins: £13 (11.6%)
Profit if trap/horse number 2 wins: £8 (7.1%)
Profit if trap/horse number 3 wins: £13 (11.6%)
Profit if trap/horse number 4 wins: £10 (8.9%)
Profit if trap/horse number 5 wins: £7 (6.2%)
Profit if trap/horse number 6 wins: £8 (7.1%)

Given that this race is contested by just six horses or greyhounds, you might imagine the amount of potential profit that can be realised in twenty-five runner handicaps, when the percentages which protect bookmakers are much higher. The example offered is one that bookmakers will contest, as these perfect books rarely, if ever, occur. The opportunity to explain a book had to be offered however and serves as a relatively simple example for all readers to comprehend.

CHAPTER 3

Watching, Listening, Inventing

Confucius made an observation a few years ago that was translated into something like, 'One see is worth a thousand hears'!

The great man could have been talking horse racing in all honesty, as you should learn straightaway to trust your eyes far more than anything you might hear relating to the sport. You will soon discover the people that are worth listening to but more often than not, the best advice is to watch closely and form your own conclusion. I should have used this policy myself many years ago, when along with my friend Lindsay Scott-Patton I became a bookmaker.

Lindsay and I opened a betting shop on the Great West Road in Brentford, Middlesex on the opening day of the Cheltenham Festival in 1978 and, like most bookmakers in those days, we were dependent on the Extel service that was in operation. We were light years from television screens at that time, along with all the technology that has aided the sport ever since. There was no early price industry as such, aside from ante-post betting relating to the main races on the calendar. The tissue men were worth their weight in gold back in the halcyon days of compiling odds and the industry waited on their every word before prices were formed.

The on course bookmakers were the first to receive the information from the tissue compilers and word of mouth whispers gradually sent the news around from region to region. Betting shops offered prices to the public just minutes before a race, punters having just the Sporting Life newspaper guidelines to aid them in their quest to beat the layers. Day after day, we would chalk up the odds relayed through the Extel service, trying to fend off the burglars who would always be looking for a back price. Back prices were those on offer before the latest show and professional con men existed up and down the land, attempting to beat the system.

These punters might have had the word that certain horses were likely to be backed on course and the said punters already had slips written out, ready to pounce on an unsuspecting cashier, pleading for the price that the punter had just missed. Security was not very tight in those days and these burglars got away with murder, as far as over the odds prices were concerned, though as greedy merchants, they were betting far too frequently to make a profit on a day to day basis. I knew several such punters and to a man they all went skint but the thrill of the chase was part of their pleasure and, if they were honest, they knew that their attitude lacked professionalism to gain a living from their supposed but illegal edge.

When a horse tightened up in the betting, there was 'Flashman' at the speed of light looking to obtain the previous price that had been available. Equally, there was the same punter in the pub after racing, scouring the Evening Standard for potential coups the next day, barely able to afford half a pint of bitter. The difference between a chain of betting shops and the individual layer should have dictated that Great West Racing (we were so inventive with names in those days) had something to offer that the main bookmakers could not afford to attract. As an individual layer, a bookmaker knows his liability immediately when a bet is struck, which is not the case for companies that have two or more outlets.

Although not wishing to let punters know, bookmakers lived in fear of well-constructed gambles in those days, as, for all they knew, multiple shops could have been the subject of a major coup several times over. As the licence holders of just one shop, why were Lindsay and I just as worried as that multiple bookmaker by what the punter might or might not know? Laying a horse to a few quid was never going to be the difference between survival and failure, so why were we panicking and acting like amateur layers?

It's a similar scenario down the line at the course, where bookies could be mistaken for window cleaners as they wash their boards down at the mere thought of being caught out by a punter with an eye for value. Boards are rubbed off to this day, irrespective of whether a joint has laid the horse that has been the subject of a gamble. The whole point of bookmaking is to accept bets though, to this day, the industry is famous for knocking back punters.

As I pointed out earlier, Lindsay and I opened our shop in 1978, four years after the 'Gay Future' affair, which took out several thousands of pounds from collective wagers up and down the country. Permit trainer Anthony Collins declared Gay Future to run in a novice hurdle at Cartmel on August Bank Holiday Monday, 1974. On the morning of the race, Gay Future was laid in doubles and trebles by staff that did not detect that something was amiss. The other two horses that formed the rest of the wager were withdrawn however and all the bets went onto Gay Future who won by 15 lengths at 10-1.

Lindsay and I should have understood the example that shops were only hit collectively, because as the stakes were relatively low, single units (bookmakers) did not suffer to any great degree. Another horse (Flockton Grey) landed another coup for informed punters four years later but these winning gambles are few and far between. Any amount of coups might have gone undetected since those gambles 20 or more years ago but because the horses in question were beaten, we will never know the real truth!

I stood as a bookmaker at Ramsgate Greyhound Stadium many years later and standing at a dog track can be one of the scariest ways to make a living in the business. One 'live' dog springs to mind when we four bookies were taken to the cleaners one Thursday night. All I remember about the dog in question is that it was as dark as the black trap four jacket that it wore... and the rest is history. The burglars were based at one of the London tracks, it might have been Hackney as I recall, and they made off with their swag amidst howls of laughter.

When there are only four joints laying prices, it is impossible to lay off the liability to any great degree and all four layers were praying for a result in the next race, for fear that the Racing Manager would be brought into play, as punters could not be paid out on winning bets by the collective bookmakers! We left by the back door as I recall, though that's another story entirely!

Had the situation occurred in a shop of course, we could have laid off the bet with any number of willing bookmakers and that's one of many reasons that Lindsay and I should have been more competitive when our respective backs were against the wall.

The word accountant comes into play yet again but as suggested earlier in the chapter, the name of the game is accepting bets by and large and that will invariably include horses or greyhounds that have been laid out to win a race. I will make an exception in the case of horses trained by the infamous Barney Curley but the majority of other supposed coups go astray and bookmakers often find themselves cursing their own lack of bottle.

Lindsay and I at Great West Racing made the mistake of treating each day as a different business. We would curse our luck if the final event of the day went against us, spoiling good figures that were in the making, yet we would shrug our shoulders if the same scenario occurred on the opening event the next day. As a business, there was no difference in the result whatsoever and we simply should have looked at the bigger picture from day one. This is where psychology rears its ugly head again because, from a positive viewpoint, a financial loss in the opening event can be overturned by results from sporting activity later that day. By losing on the last race, we were psychologically beaten. We used to be a miserable pair of numpties in the pub following racing, if that last race had gone the way of the punters.

I remember going up to the head office one evening as a betting shop manager many years before, when the boss, Johnny White, asked me how the shop had performed on the day. I suggested that the last result was our undoing, having been well ahead half way through the afternoon. Johnny asked me what I meant by the term 'last race' and

I took little time to explain what I thought was the correct answer. He suggested to me that there was no such thing as the last race, as such an event was the first race on the next day's card, or in some cases, the first race at Walthamstow dogs that same night. I was too young to appreciate his answer in all honesty but I know what Johnny meant now!

I mentioned the legendary Freddie Williams in the foreword and I would hazard a guess that it is this part of the book that might attract his interest. Looking back on results is probably not part of his agenda and the Williams' team will continually strive to make a living by being bold, which is something to behold in the betting jungle. One of the most frightening times during my long association within the trade, was when our joint was the only book to turn up at Ramsgate one evening... which occurred on a 'busy' Saturday night! Fortunately the night in question was during the winter and only the locals were in evidence.

That fact did not detract from the point that chalking up prices in front of punters who took the form guide more seriously than life itself is a perilous business, especially when there are no laying off facilities on offer. We would have paid the earth for the mobile phone business to have been in place at the time but then again, so much activity in greyhound betting takes place in the final 60 seconds before the traps rise, there would not have been time to get on the blower anyway! The joint made a small profit on the night as I remember, though it was probably the lowest rate of pay I have ever made on an hourly basis.

Freddie and his team enter a serious fray on a regular basis and the way that they accept monumental bets ensures that the laying off scenario is rarely accommodated. The figures that the Williams' team attracts would make my Great

West and Ramsgate days seem like a game of Escalado but I guess that a fiver to me might equate to a thousand to you, or ten pence as the case might be.

Invention is a swear word in the ears of many bookmakers, yet the layers forget that if they had just laid single bets down the years, many of them would have disappeared many years ago. Doubles, trebles etc were invented by the bookmaker for the bookmaker, not for the benefit of punters, who can be so naïve at times. The lucky 15 wager has become very popular over the last ten years or so and many punters are still taken in by this bet, believing the bookmakers to be generous because of the various bonuses on offer for the potential investor. The point that the naïve client fails to spot is that the concession of offering punters money back for one winner is a marketing ploy that punters just cannot comprehend.

The bet of a yankee plus four singles has been in evidence for many years and the wager was known as a yap in the old days.

One of the bookmakers eventually decided to offer a bonus of doubling the price of a single winner to lure clients into staking the bet and old Joe Soap and his pals fell for it hook, line and sinker.

Bookmakers were onto a winner on two fronts. Initially, the marketing channelled the unsuspecting client into staking an additional 36% compared to their previous daily wager of eleven bets (yankee), whilst the icing on the cake was the bookmakers ploy of luring the punter into the shop the next day, with just the one winner.

The psychology involved with the bookmaker was nothing short of brilliant, because many punters would give their daily bet the elbow for a while if they were not backing winners. By offering a return for just one winner however, the layer was luring the client back into their lair in order to entice more money out of their unsuspecting victim. The bookmaker could offer all types of bonuses for four winners on the betting slip, because such occurrences were few and far between. I couldn't possibly estimate the number of bets that I have settled that included every winner on a slip from four selections upwards but, at a wild guess, it would be far less than one tenth of one percent.

Psychology has played a massive part in the war between bookmaker and punter down the years, as terrestrial television has proved. How many punters have geared their Saturday wager towards the live racing on the box, irrespective of the races in question? These contests include some of the toughest puzzles punters have to solve but cashiers are never so busy than when bookmakers offer 7/1 the field for a big race on a Saturday. Why else do you think that bookmakers started to sponsor handicap races, luring owners and trainers to declare horses, making the race a lottery as far as punters were concerned week on week? Television punters are geared towards betting on many races instead of the odd one or two and clients carry the negative psychology into work with them during the week.

Clients hurry into a betting shop during their lunch hour and scribble down four horses, even though the last couple of selections are often added simply to make up the required numbers for the relevant wager. Having managed betting shops for many years when people actually stepped over the threshold to bet, rather than play machines, I can verify that the most popular bet was a yankee and latterly the lucky 15.

Cunning traps had been successfully laid by bookmakers marketing multiple bets, suggesting to punters that investors could win many thousands of pounds for small stakes. How different this was to the legal scenario even well into the seventies, when shops could not use the word 'try' in their marketing efforts.

In the days of the old black/whiteboards it was illegal to use such a phrase as 'Try a lucky 15 today', as the bookmaker was seen to be luring the punter into placing a bet! Bookmakers have never had to try to get people to gamble in all honesty.

The yankee and lucky 15 has arguably been overtaken by the popularity of the toteplacepot (note the change of marketing by the Tote) in recent years and I can confirm the vulnerability of the punter, even as far as tote pools are concerned.

Turf racing other than Leopardstown's Irish card was wiped out by inclement weather on 28 December 2005, leaving the delights of Wolverhampton as the only venue. The Tote would have expected to attract a toteplacepot pool of around £35,000 on all weather racing on a Wednesday in December, yet the figure in question reached £108,116.

The Art of Bookmaking is to have something on offer for the public to gamble on, preferably a televised event. The fact that Wolverhampton was available free to air on At The Races, as opposed to fee-paying Racing UK clients was a vital factor in producing the oversized toteplacepot pool. The fact that the Lingfield all weather toteplacepot pool totalled over £107,000 the next day proves my point.

The invention of bets for the horse racing sector has increased of late, though not as much I would have liked, speaking on behalf of the public. Match betting has become available in recent times through head to head betting between two horses in a race. This attracts the larger investor by and large and I would like the layers to extend this principle to additional runners in some of the top handicaps. With twenty runners and more protecting the bookmaker's margins on a regular basis, some discerning customers choose to ignore such contests in the belief that these events are impossible to predict. Even John McCririck has relayed news that the betting ring has been quiet on such occasions, so isn't it about time that some of the bookmakers offered the public more opportunities to play?

I advise my sportinglife.com readers to consider choosing one horse from each part of the draw for their toteplacepot investments in big handicap events, hoping to at least get a run for their money.

Using the same principle, why can't the bookmakers divide a race up utilising the low and high numbers in the draw? It's all well and good the layers complaining that they have lost trade through the exchanges but the time has come to fight back by offering the type of markets that will attract punters back to basic, old fashioned betting.

Using the 2005 starting prices for the Lincoln Handicap as an example, bookmakers could have priced up the following horses in a revised market as follows.

Low drawn runners:

Draw	Name	SP	Revised Betting	Finishing Position
1	Resplendent One	28/1	10/1	SECOND
2	Common World	14/1	5/1	WON
3	Rocket Force	100/1	33/1	unplaced
4	Vortex	16/1	11/2	THIRD
5	St Petersburg	12/1	4/1	unplaced
6	Divine Gift	8/1	5/2 fav	unplaced
7	Mine	20/1	7/1	unplaced
8	Polygonal	18/1	6/1	unplaced

Those drawn high:

Draw	Name	SP	Revised Betting	Finishing Position
22	Forever Free	100/1	33/1	unplaced
21	New Seeker	15/2	2/1	WON
20	Cardinal Venture	40/1	14/1	unplaced
19	Appalachian Trail	18/1	11/2	THIRD
18	My Paris	25/1	17/2	unplaced
17	Jazz Scene	16/1	5/1	unplaced
16	Kings Thought	40/1	14/1	unplaced
15	Blythe Knight	9/1	5/2	SECOND

Potential layers might take the opinion that the horses nearest the rail on either side of the track could have been shortened in price, whilst those drawn nearer the middle could have balanced the books in terms of odds. Either way, there is surely room for manoeuvre and whilst the bookmakers might moan about decreasing percentages, they have to ask themselves one question; do they want to be in business or perhaps be players themselves?

For this example, I have offered the revised prices based on starting prices, hopefully showing that the situation would have been a winner from a marketing perspective.

So how was the revised betting evaluated?

Arithmetic once again comes to the fore, as the first job is to establish the percentages, using the starting prices, that the runners equal in total.

Using the high number scenario as the example, the total sum was 42.5%. (1.0 + 11.7 + 2.4 + 5.3 + 3.8 + 5.9 + 2.4 + 10.0).

Offering bookmakers a decent deal by creating a book of 120.9%, the next move is to divide the 120.9 by the resulting 42.5, which equates to 2.84.

Now multiply the percentage for each of the eight runners by 2.84 to determine the relevant prices.

I have rounded each runner up or down to the nearest respective prices to bring the book to exactly 120.9%.

Because of the nature of this revised market, I have slightly reduced the price of the outsiders, which most bookmakers would appreciate. With the prospect of jockeys failing to ride out a finish if their mounts were well beaten at the time, the each way market becomes dangerous for the layer and though some bookmakers might like this idea in principle, they might decide to offer a win only book. This option would still prove attractive to punters in my considered opinion, provided the layers were generous with their prices, perhaps betting to as little as 112.9%. You will come to appreciate the 0.9% at the end of the percentage figures as a potential bookmaker when you read through this publication.

I also appreciate that layers would ideally have put ten runners into the equation, especially from an each way 'bet to nothing' perspective and that is their prerogative. All I'm suggesting is that the public are offered more opportunities. As the Wolverhampton toteplacepot example showed earlier, punters are out there willing to gamble their cash if the bookmakers offer clients something to bet on, especially when the public don't feel they are being taken for a ride. Less complicated bets, to accommodate punters that are staring the bookmakers in the face, include two potential wagers on the football front.

Take the 2006 World Cup Finals as an example. The layers continued to ignore the unbiased punter who simply wanted an interest in any given game, preferably with some value attached.

Correct score betting is one of the most popular of wagers in this sector of the industry and, with a little more imagination from the layers, the revenue could increase still further. Matches that do not affect England during the competition can be a turn off for some punters, so why don't bookmakers offer an incentive for punters to bet with their company as opposed to the opposition down the road? Let's take the Switzerland v South Korea match, from the opposite half of the draw to England, as an example.

Bookmakers might price up 1-0 victories for either side at 6/1 and 7/1 respectively (Switzerland victory odds quoted first).

In a game that might not attract a great deal of business, why not offer either side to win 1-0 at 3/1 (or 10/3 if the layer is really generous) about prices that equate to 11/4 when added together?

Far more speculative bets are offered later on in the

book but this is a basic idea that could surely illustrate that bookmakers are intent on attracting new clients by way of a little generosity towards potential punters. The attraction to this idea for bookmakers (as opposed to others in this publication) is that there is no new invention involved, just a variation on a theme that already works.

Similarly, in an example that reverts back to the bread and butter league fixtures, why can't bookmakers be bold enough to offer ante-post bets on games beyond the matches that are priced up for the next weekend? As an odds compiler, I was conditioned to have my prices ready for games that related to midweek matches beyond the Saturday fixtures. On a Saturday morning in the office, I might have a potential midweek league game priced up as follows:

Evs Manchester United
9/4 The Draw
9/4 Arsenal

Because of printing deadlines in those days, as a company we had to fax over our prices at five o'clock, so that coupons could be delivered Monday/Tuesday the following week. Depending on the results on the Saturday, I might have tweaked the prices a little before five o'clock to read 11/10 Man Utd and 2/1 Arsenal, if the afternoon results had faired better for Arsenal than United.

If I could be prepared to have such prices ready in the old days when there was no online activity, why can't bookmakers try and attract more business by betting beyond the next game when they have technology on their side?

Punters are continually being asked to forecast results using ante-post betting relating to the sport of kings, yet the bookmakers seemingly haven't got the bottle (because of the three – home, draw or away – result scenario) to price up football games in advance. Why not offer prices for the fictitious Man United v Arsenal game before the weekend matches have been played?

Without the cost of printing coupons, bookmakers could at least offer this service to online clients, even if the layers reverted back to the dark days by possibly offering a maximum of three selections per line. In the bad old days, bookmakers demanded that punters make at least three selections per line, whereby punters could not bank on individual teams.

This move would allow punters to invest in singles, doubles and a treble (given three matches on offer), which would minimise potential damage for bookmakers. When the going gets tough, the tough get going, or so we are led to believe and bookmakers need to show this type of attitude if they are to remain in business, or at least stop complaining about lost revenue to the exchanges. Punters would appreciate that the layers were fighting for business and the competition for wagers could only increase revenue for the industry as a whole.

Put truthfully, there is no reason why this attitude could not be adopted. It is time for the bookmakers to stop crying and offer punters the opportunity to invest in speculative bets from both a laying and backing perspective. There is no reason why backing and laying has to be viewed as betting exchange terminology alone.

'Jolly Joe' was an on-course layer in the south that I admired a few decades ago. Joe had one of those booming voices that would make John McCririck sound quiet and his invention was to offer odds on a daily double basis. The Tote ran the official 'Tote Double' in those days to a fifty pence (ten shillings) stake and whether or not Joe was in direct competition to those races I cannot recall. What I do know, however, is that Joe priced up the two most competitive races on the card in most instances and offered odds accordingly. This was a bookmaker who knew the game inside out, because he wasn't looking to attract the larger wagers that might have been flying around Sandown Park on a summer's afternoon, not at least until he had some money in the hod. Joe was more intent on laying the ten-shilling bet to all and sundry early doors, happy to cream off his potential margin in the process.

There were unquestionably more mug punters in those days and, just for the thrill of the chase, I lined up to join the ranks from time to time.

Joe would start betting on his daily double a full hour before the first race and would continue doing so between early races on the card, bearing in mind that the most competitive events usually occur around the half way mark at a meeting. Joe was obviously hoping to enjoy a clean bill of health after the first leg but even given a bad result, he could afford to offset the running up liabilities in the concluding event. I thought his stance was every bit as impressive as when John Banks handed out the ice creams to children, who then told mum and dad to go and bet with that nice bookie! Those days at the track are long gone unfortunately, with just the growling Barry Dennis offering his wares as a poor substitute!

The game isn't easy in all honesty and I've even seen some of the top independent joints having to take money on the next race in order to pay out on the previous event. Such circumstances are not as uncommon as you might believe. If the layers are more inventive, however, there is still room for the brave to flourish.

Jolly Joe's stance was impressive because he looked to the lower end of the scale for his bread and butter business, a start to the day whereby his ledger was filling up whilst others were bare.

Joe was also avoiding the 'sweets', where hungry layers priced up their boards early, only for the sharks to close in when an error had been made. Experienced racegoers based south of Watford will remember the Power brothers who stood at the Hackney, Walthamstow and Wembley dog tracks years ago.

Tom was the less volatile of the pair but nothing enraged the man more than when his fellow bookmakers acted unprofessionally in his (correct) opinion. I was a regular at Walthamstow in those halcyon days and Tom would take a mental note of the highest prices on offer for the six greyhounds in question and then berate his fellow layers after the race. The other layers seemed intent to accommodate punters, knocking out prices too early, only for the bigger players, who were biding their time to come in for the kill, to home in on the bookmakers as the greyhounds were being loaded into the traps.

Time and again the bookmakers were betting over broke but whilst the opposing bookmakers seemed happy to accommodate the punters at any price, Tom would stomp off to the bar between races in a foul mood. Tom was going there to drink, maybe the odd whisky but not often, he was there to purchase another cigar and to moan about his fellow layers! He would point to me on occasions and shout, 'I suppose you told them to lay those odds!'

I priced up Tom's football coupon at Upton Park back in those days, offering potential bets that were different to those seen at other grounds.

He rarely paid me for the work but then again, my losing account was never paid as I recall! Tom was also in the bar to wind the punters up, particularly after a race when the layers had beaten the opposition. He would strut around like a demented cockerel, damning punters who dared to take him on. It was Tom's way of securing business, as he taunted punters to try their luck in the next event. His brother John was warned off at Huntingdon after a bar brawl as I remember, which is as good a description as I can offer about one of the most interesting joints during the seventies and eighties. Despite his booming voice, Jolly Joe was not a volatile type by comparison. He just shared the Power's belief that there are more ways of filling up a ledger than being the first one up with prices that only attract the silver ring merchants and live money.

Joe's daily double book was over round in the extreme but he was offering a decent return for punters against small investments, which is more than can be said for betting on the distance merchants that can still be found on course. Some of these books are 40 or 50% over round on occasions, as unsuspecting punters wager their hard earned cash on what they perceive as being an interesting alternative to the basic odds on offer down the line, particularly in events that are dominated by a long odds on shot. Nobody is forcing the punter's arm, I agree, but it's time that these bandits were run out of town for the benefit of the game in general. The odds on offer at these joints are not inventive. They are geared towards taking an uneducated public for granted and have no place in an industry that is trying to attract people to come racing.

Conversely, an inventive bookmaker might attract business by offering a money back guarantee if an outsider happened to prevail in a particular race. When you consider that a 66/1 chance relates to 1.5% of the book, could it be considered dangerous for a layer to advertise that all monies taken on an event (perhaps up to a maximum of fifty pounds) would be repaid in the event of a nominated rag winning the race? How abhorrent is that for bookmakers to digest, against the argument from the punter's perspective that all bets are lost if a horse refuses to race?

I suggest that the two potential scenarios occur as frequently as each other, so why shouldn't the punter bet on a level playing field with a bookmaker who has the bottle to offer such a service?

Other opportunities are limited on course nowadays thanks to computerised receipts, otherwise I would have suggested that dutching could be accommodated on course. There is no reason why this scenario could not be offered in shops, however. Why lay one horse when, for the sake of being generous (slightly better coupled odds), you can lay two?

Given two 6/1 chances for example, equates to 5/2, isn't there a chance that you will lay a thicker bet at slightly inflated odds of 11/4 compared to a couple of single bets at 6/1?

Bets could be subject to a maximum win of £100 as an example and, by the way, I'm not suggesting that all these inventive bets would be laid on the same day. Turf accountancy is the name of the game and I have not lost sight that the business is governed by numbers, the majority of which, as a bookmaker, you want on your side.

My mind wanders back to a fried breakfast I frequently ate during the seventies and no, I have not drunk too much sauce at the time of writing! I used to frequent a greasy spoon in Ealing, which attracted black cab drivers like you have never seen.

The proprietor was a canny chap named Tony, and a mate suggested I should pay the café a visit next time that I was in the area, without telling me the reason why. I soon realised why the premises were so busy, having taken into account the pictures of film stars and footballers that adorned every inch of space on the walls. At any given time, Tony would announce that there was a free sausage sandwich for the first person to correctly answer an up and coming question.

Don't ask me what the questions were some thirty years later but I can confirm that the competition was fierce. The questions were based on his two loves of football and the movies and Tony was a well-read sort of chap. Even if he was mistaken from time to time, Tony's word was final! Tony's rules suggested that no one person could win two prizes on any given day and that Smart Alec's who were looking to spoil the party by shouting out the answer if they had already won a free mug of tea or any of the variety of prizes would be barred for the week.

Given the inventive wagers and ideas that I offer in this publication, Tony would have made a great bookmaker, believing that a full shop or café offering a small percentage of profit back to the clients, is infinitely preferable to half empty premises.

CHAPTER 4

Horse Racing

The sport of kings must take centre stage as far as this book is concerned, as horse racing is the bread and butter of the business.

For all that punters moan about trainers and jockeys from time to time, horse racing attracts thousands into shops up and down the land on a daily basis.

People have occasional, speculative bets on the dogs but when a punter picks up their daily newspaper in the morning, they generally cast their eyes up and down the racecards first and foremost. Why are punters attracted to the hardest races on the card? Furthermore, why do bookmakers like these handicaps so much? Not only do these handicaps produce some of the most frenzied and varied gambles during the course of the year but the handicapper has done much of the work on the bookmaker's behalf, attempting to create a multiple dead heat in the process.

Compare the scenario of pricing up a handicap, to a three-year-old maiden event at Thirsk, with several of the top trainers involved.

Some horses will come into the maiden as debutantes, whilst others boast uncertain form gained from all manner of venues and ground conditions. A Newmarket trainer might have sent a (whispered) horse to contest the event, whilst there is always the draw to consider at the various venues.

Handicappers, outside of nursery events for two-year-olds, will invariably have form on both left and right-handed tracks and have probably carried all type of weights whilst acting on different types of going. All of these situations aid the handicapper and the bookmaker alike when they are analysing a potential handicap event. Bookmakers are therefore armed with all sorts of information in a competitive looking handicap compared to a maiden event and the layers welcome money from punters who are trying to solve the puzzle. Once the handicapper had made his judgement, the odds compilers run their respective eyes over the field from an ante-post perspective, looking for potential springers in any market they might price up.

Horses trained by Barney Curley and the like (Reg Akehurst in the old days) would be kept on the right side, as would any young horse that was beginning to run up a sequence of decent performances or victories.

It's as well to consider greyhound racing at this stage, because when pricing up a graded event, the equivalent of a handicap to a fashion, would you rather be on the side of an experienced runner that has forgotten how to win, or a young pup that is progressing through the grades at a rate of knots? A good example, aside from the maiden and handicap scenarios, of the problems of pricing up a race, was the 2005 renewal of Wetherby's Castleford Chase which was contested on December 27. The race was a particularly difficult contest to gauge, despite the fact that just five runners faced the starter.

Oneway was returned as the 5/4 favourite, despite the

fact that outside of two victories at Sandown (his favourite track), Mark Rimell's raider had won two races in each of the 'D' and 'E' categories and this was a Grade Two event!

The proximity of his 'Tingle Creek' effort against Kauto Star and Ashley Brook (beaten one and a half lengths and eight), presumably led to the short price of the return on this occasion.

Oneway had finished in front of Monkerhostin, who had only been beaten in a photo-finish by Kicking King in the 'King George' the day prior to the Wetherby event. It all added up to a good effort being on the cards in the Castleford Chase. In hindsight, it's as well to dwell on the fact that the 'Tingle Creek' event is staged at Sandown, which is possibly the reason for Oneway's proximity to Kauto Star and Ashley Brook.

The second favourite for the Wetherby event was Fundamentalist (drifted from 2/1 to 3/1), who was coming into the race as a potential champion over anything from the minimum trip to three miles plus but had been off the track for a year following an injury after some first class efforts. As an 11/2 chance, Mister McGoldrick was attempting to win his seventh race at Wetherby from just eight starts, whilst Albuhera (6/1) was representing the all-conquering yard of Paul Nicholls, who was to saddle the first three home in the Welsh National on the same day.

The field was made up by 12/1 chance El Vaquero, saddled by Howard Johnson, who had trained three winners on Boxing Day.

As winners of an aggregate of 32 out of 94 races before flag-fall, this was a quality field that tested the skill of the tissue workers.

With the Betfair market not quite as informative as usual

because of the bank holiday scenario, this market was particularly difficult to assess. The prevailing tacky ground basically put Fundamentalist out of the equation and, in hindsight, course specialist Mister McGoldrick was a decent bet to nothing wager from an each way perspective and Sue Smith's raider proved the point, scoring by a dozen lengths.

It's easy to speak after the event of course, especially as the winner was all of ten pounds the wrong way with Oneway in the official figures, which is another reason that the favourite was sent off at a skinny price. Mister McGoldrick was rated four pounds inferior to Oneway but had to concede six pounds to the favourite on this occasion. As a stats man, I also had to consider that the trainer of Mister McGoldrick, Sue Smith, was on the cold list having trained over 50 consecutive losers prior to this event.

In hindsight, El Vaquero could easily have been dismissed on the grounds that Howard Johnson's raider had never tackled a race over the minimum trip, whereby his jockey was duty bound to try and slip his field, which is never easy at a venue like Wetherby with its testing fences.

On a day that traditionally produces shock results however (as was the case on this day – Inglis Drever and Moscow Flyer were both beaten), layers could hardly push El Vaquero further out in the market. In contrast to El Vaquero, the eventual runner up Albuhera had won seven of his eight races over 17 furlongs or less and bearing in mind the uncertainty of the fitness of Fundamentalist and the lack of experience in decent races (away from Sandown) of the favourite, both the first and second horses home could have been utilised in a dutching combination.

By effectively backing both Mister McGoldrick and

Albuhera at SP, you were taking odds of 12/5 about the pair in a level stake scenario. Alternatively, exchange players would suggest that you could simply have laid the favourite if you thought he was too short a price, along with Fundamentalist, when adverse ground conditions had become apparent.

Reverting back to starting prices, this is where the basics of percentages come into play, because although we are talking after the event, ask yourself one question if you remember the race in detail. Did Oneway really hold a 44.4% chance of winning that Grade Two event? Whatever your answer to that question might be, you will hopefully understand what the bookmaker was asked to evaluate before putting chalk to board, in just one of six races on that Wetherby card.

Taking the three race examples (a competitive handicap, the Thirsk maiden event and the Castleford Chase), which one would you rather price up as a bookmaker?

Consider the Castleford Chase against a five-furlong event for two-year-olds at Windsor, just after the start of a new flat season. Only two of the juveniles have racing experience and racecourse whispers in this example are few and far between. How does the odds compiler do its work, some twenty-eight hours in advance of the race?

Here are the runners, trainers and eventual prices that I determined after a good deal of thought.

Horse A – trained by Milton Bradley – 25/1
Horse B – trained by Mick Channon – 11/4
Horse C – trained by Richard Hannon – 5/2
Horse D – trained by Barry Hills – 4/1
Horse E – trained by Bill Muir – 16/1

Horse F – trained by Michael Jarvis – 9/2
Horse G – trained by Clive Brittain – 14/1
Horse H – trained by Chris Wall – 16/1

The eight prices equate to a 115.7% book.

Readers might suggest that an over round book of 15.7% fails to offer punters any value but the bookmakers have to defend themselves in what is a 'dead eight' contest, albeit mythical. The 'sharks' would soon be circling around the books if any of the front four in the market touches 5/1, the 'bet to nothing' from an each way perspective.

The prices were offered for the following reasons:

Horse A – Best draw (10) in the field on this good going but little else to recommend him. Trainer's record last year with debutant was 0/11 and all three juvenile raiders at the track in 2005 were beaten.

Horse B – Mick Channon's raider was third on his debut in a reasonable race but although Mick saddled fifty-four two-year-old winners last year, his record was 0/11 at Windsor. However, bookmakers discount Mick's juveniles at their peril.

Horse C – Saddling a pivotal debutant, Richard Hannon had ten juvenile winners at the track in 2005 and six of his two-year-olds won at the first time of asking last year.

Horse D – Nothing special in terms of breeding or yearling fee, the Barry Hills raider is representing a stable that saddled five debutant winners last year (twenty-seven juvenile winners in total), whilst boasting a 1/5 record at Windsor.

Horse E – Bill Muir is amongst the two-year-old winners already this term and one of his nine winners last year was successful at this venue. However, most of Bill's juvenile winners would not be taking on this class of runner.

Horse F – Unplaced when showing promise only seven days ago, this was an £80,000 yearling but Michael Jarvis was 0/7 with his Windsor juveniles last year and the Piccolo gelding has the worst of the draw in trap one. 9/2 is a sensible price to offer in the circumstances, protecting the each way ledger.

Horse G – Clive Brittain, with one debutant winner on forty-four juveniles last year, saddles a King's Best gelding that is bred to get a mile before too long, even in his first season. All three of Clive's juvenile raiders were beaten here last year.

Horse H – Chris Wall is not known as a prolific trainer of two-year-olds and this newcomer has it all to do from his stall two draw. Chris saddled five unsuccessful juveniles at this venue last year and the trend will continue here, likely as not.

If I was betting from a win only perspective, trying to attract more trade, I might consider offering the following odds; in order: 28/1 – 11/4 – 5/2 – 9/2 – 18/1 – 5/1 – 16/1 – 18/1 which would create a 110.1% book.

This two-year-old race is a hypothetical example, with the 2006 turf form conjured from my imagination.

A real race to use as another example was the Skybet Chase at Southwell in January and, in offering advice after the result was known, I'll try and be as honest in my assessment as possible. The winner, A Glass In Thyne was returned at 16/1, which was certainly as big a price as I was likely to offer, given the fact that the previous five winners had carried weights of 10-12 or less in the race. Only the fourth horse home, Our Armageddon, carried less weight than the 10-12 that A Glass In Thyne humped to victory, though each way supporters of Our Armageddon would have been frustrated by the withdrawal of the sixteenth runner in the field prior to flag fall.

A Glass In Thyne was only contesting the sixth race of his career and just the fourth over fences; I guess his inexperience was the main reason for the generous return.

Bookmakers sent off two joint favourites at 9/2, with a coupled price of 7/4 and, though Mark Pitman's Too Forward traveled well for most of the race, the 11-8 burden was anchoring the ten-year-old when push came to shove in the home straight.

Andrew Thornton set the winner alight two fences from home and on good to soft ground, horses in his wake struggled to change gear after a good pace from the outset.

The other joint market leader King Harald was on a retrieving mission having disappointed this season after showing a deal of potential the previous year. King Harald unseated his rider five fences from home.

In hindsight, bookmakers could argue that 9/2 was a reasonable quote about the market leader in this type of race, as the previous five favourites had been sent off at 100/30 (14 ran) − 4/1 (12) − 3/1 (18) − 15/8 (12) − 4/1 (11). Punters might have argued that just one favourite has scored during the period, with one other placed jolly.

I would have shortened up the four nine-year-olds in the field, as the three previous renewals had all been won by that age of horse.

Six-year-old Aristoxene was on offer at 10/1 fromNicky Henderson's Lambourn stable, though 16/1 would have been nearer my mark, given the fact that only one horse had finished in the frame of ten six and seven-year-old representatives during the study period.

Keltic Bard (another lightly raced individual) finished third at 14/1, which looked about right from a layer's perspective, though Charlie Mann's raider was going as well as anything turning for home. I guess the 11-6 burden eventually caught up with the nine-year-old who was offered as short as 3/1 in running.

Europa split the first and third horses home and, unlike the aforementioned individuals, Ferdy Murphy's raider was thoroughly exposed but did well stepping back in trip to this three mile contest. As a ten-year-old, Europa was representing a vintage that was claiming its sixth toteplacepot position in the last five years and 16/1 was a generous return, given the five-pound claim that young Dreaper was allowed in the saddle.

I might not have been as fair as the bookmakers about last year's winner, Colourful Life from the Paul Nicholls yard, who was allowed to go off at 8/1, despite the fact that the brilliant young claimer Liam Heard reduced the burden to 11-1. The layers were right however, as the ten-year-old was never really travelling and a bad mistake put paid to his chances some way from home.

Jakari was third favourite for the event and Henry Daly's raider might have been a little unlucky, as he was badly hampered at a vital stage of the race. Whether he would have found as much as the winner in the straight, however, is open to doubt. The bookmakers were bullish against Martin Pipe's pair, Polar Red and Horus, probably because of the poor form of the stable representatives at the time, coupled with the fact that both horses were shadows of their former selves by the time this race was contested.

Sonevafushi went off at 13/2 but was always going

to struggle to last home, having set a strong pace when carrying 11-12, whilst outsiders Royal Emperor, Scots Grey and Mixsterthetrixster were all pulled up having been outclassed.

Starting prices – with my prices in brackets:

9/2 Too Forward (5/1)
9/2 King Harald (11/2)
11/2 Jakari (5/1)
13/2 Sonevafushi (13/2)
8/1 Colourful Life (13/2)
10/1 Aristoxene (16/1)
14/1 Keltic Bard (14/1)
16/1 A Glass In Thyne (14/1)
16/1 Europa (14/1)
20/1 Our Armageddon (16/1)
25/1 Royal Emperor (33/1)
33/1 Scots Grey (33/1)
50/1 Mixsterthetrixster (40/1)
50/1 Polar Red (33/1)
50/1 Horus (33/1)

Further reasons for the prices I would have offered (betting to 127.7% compared to SP figures of 124.4%).

I would not have been so generous with the prices for the extreme outsiders, given the unproven form of the market leaders leading up to the race. King Harald was the ante-post favourite, despite having looked drunk on the run in at Cheltenham after a mistake at the last of his seasonal debut, which was followed by a poor effort in the Hennessy when pulled up. Joint favourite Too Forward was the pick of the pair, in my humble opinion but, for all his talent as a trainer, Mark Pitman struggled to get his horses to put together a consistent run of good efforts.

Europa came into the race having been placed in just one of his eight recent efforts, whilst A Glass In Thyne and Keltic Bard were the possible improvers in the event, having been lightly raced for different reasons. Jakari had to be kept on the right side, with six victories and five other placed efforts from a twenty-race career in the winter game.

Colourful Life had been beaten in all five races since his victory in this event twelve months ago but four of those races were the William Hill Chase at the Festival, the Scottish National, The 'Charlie Hall' and Newbury's Hennessy Gold Cup. In his only other start, Colourful Life had been beaten little more than a length on his seasonal debut at Chepstow in October in a class two event and the winner of that race, I Hear Thunder, went on to score next time out.

I'm often asked the question as a stats anorak, whether the bookmakers take account of the type of information I seek in my quest to beat the bookmaker as a punter? As a former odds complier, I can assure you that bookmakers leave no stone unturned in their war against the enemy, although the type of stats that I produce (particularly relating to trends in certain races) would not be uppermost in their thoughts. Bookmakers would tend to suggest that trends (like rules) are there to be broken and the 2005 renewal of the Hennessy Gold Cup is a good argument from that viewpoint.

Horses down towards the bottom of the weights had dominated the event leading up to the race in question, yet the first four horses home (Trabolgan – L'Ami – Cornish Rebel – Comply Or Die) all hailed from the top of the weights. My immediate response to cynics at the time, was to point out that the going for the Hennessy in 2005 was decidedly better than is usually the case at Newbury at that time of year (late November to early December) and this, along with strong Sun Alliance Chase form from earlier in the year, was the main reason that the better horses eventually dominated the finish.

This is another reason for looking at all races on their respective merits and why the going is such an important factor in racing.

The Cheltenham Festival results in recent years have become easier to predict, now that good going is in evidence at Prestbury Park on the majority of occasions. Bookmakers mourn the day that the Cheltenham Executive decided that drainage work was required at Prestbury Park some years ago, because, aside from outsiders winning the lesser events in March, results have gone the way of punters in recent times.

Given the consistency of ground conditions at Lingfield (and Wolverhampton for that matter), I can't quite work out why the results are so unpredictable on the all weather surfaces. Rather than look at the age and weight trends, layers will look back at records relating to the profit or loss in certain events in the racing calendar.

The 'Champion Chase' market is in a state of confusion at the time of writing but bookmakers will not allow Kauto Star to deviate from their current quote of around the 7/4 mark, simply because the 'Tingle Creek' has become such a good marker for the championship race over the years. Kauto Star has been taken out of the 'Victor Chandler' betting at the time of writing and who can blame Paul Nicholls for this move?

The Ditcheat handler has enough cover in a race where the six-year-old was due to give upwards of seven pounds to his rivals.

Martin Pipe made one of his rare mistakes in my view last year, when he asked Well Chief to take on Azertyuiop at Newbury only a couple of weeks after David Johnson's raider had lumped top weight to an impressive victory at Cheltenham in the VC.

I'm sure this was part of Paul's thinking in withdrawing Kauto Star from this year's renewal and having been beaten just four lengths by Monkerhostin (giving the Philip Hobbs raider as many pounds) at Exeter first time up this season, Kauto Star had nothing to prove once the 'Tingle Creek' had been landed.

When considering the price of a horse as a bookmaker, a layer must also take into account the strength of the potential opposition.

Moscow Flyer had looked a shadow of his former self at the time of writing yet was next best in at 5/1, whilst the comprehensively beaten Ashley Brook (third in the betting lists) has seen the backend of 'Kauto' in his two races this season and probably required longer than the minimum trip. The bookmakers are no mugs and the shortest price of the other Irish raiders was 10/1, which might look big now in hindsight but nobody was knocking down the doors of the bookmaker's offices to secure the prices at the time.

The Tingle Creek Chase is renowned as being THE trial for the 'Queen Mother,' so Kauto Star deserved his billing at the top of the market, in my considered opinion. I thought that 7/4 was a mighty attractive price at the time of writing.

7/4 represents a percentage of 36.4% in bookmaking

terms. Did you believe that Kauto Star had a better than 36.4% chance of lifting the two mile crown at Prestbury Park back in January when this text was written?

You will probably know the result of the race by now, which puts you at an advantage. At all times as a backer or a layer, however, you must be honest with yourself, or you will go skint in double quick time.

The Leopardstown races over the Christmas period have also flagged up many an Irish Cheltenham Festival winner of late and the advice to backers and layers alike, whilst we are relating Festival opinions, is to take the form seriously, even though the going on the Thursday of that December meeting is very unlikely to be repeated at Prestbury Park in March.

Leopardstown scorers at the December meeting (in alphabetical order) were:

Back To Bid (yielding)
Beef Or Salmon (yielding to soft)
Black Apalachi (yielding to soft)
Black Harry (yielding to soft)
Brave Inca (soft)
Buck Whaley (yielding)
Celestial Wave (soft)
Clear Riposte (yielding)
Dancing Hero (soft)
Escrea (yielding to soft)
Finger on the Pulse (yielding)
Firth of Forth (soft)
Heez a Wonder (soft)
Hi Cloy (yielding to soft)
Le Coudray (yielding to soft)

Missed That (yielding)
Mr Nosie (yielding to soft)
Nickname (soft)
Rocket Ship (soft)
Rosaker (yielding to soft)
Snow Tern (yielding to soft)
Southern Vic (yielding to soft)
Sublimity (yielding to soft)
Sweet Wake (yielding to soft)
Tazmania (yielding to soft)
Vox Populi (yielding to soft)
Whitehills (yielding)
Zum See (yielding)

The other horse that should be added to the list is Central House (yielding to soft) whose jockey 'misplaced' the winning post, when allowing Hi Cloy to go on and score!

There is at least one important factor for each of the two racing codes, ignoring, as I tend to do, the all weather race-tracks.

The draw is the most simple important factor relating to flat races whilst the going is equally important under the winter code of racing. Yes, other factors do contribute but, by and large, these two areas dominate the respective sports. Winter racing over obstacles is not affected by the draw of course but both of these important factors can coincide to create chaos at a flat venue.

Imagine the scene at Windsor on a Monday evening for example.

Runners have been declared for a five furlong sprint on fast ground, with high numbers very much favoured on the stands side of the track.

The clouds gather around lunchtime and three or four hours of constant heavy drizzle rains down onto the track, eventually producing soft ground. The declared horses would have been sent to the Berkshire venue with trainers mindful that the projected ground would have suited their various representatives.

Trainers are now faced by changing ground conditions, as well as a variation from the draw bias. Non-runners begin to rear their ugly heads, for bookmakers and punters alike. A horse drawn 20 out of 20 who had overnight ground conditions in their favour, is in good form and hails from a top stable, might have been projected as the 7/2 favourite when prices were formed that morning. With the changed going and the possibility that a favourable draw has now resulted in anything but an advantage, the horse in question is now being offered at 6/1. Racegoers seem to view such circumstances as an advantage to the bookmaker, in much the same way as punters berate what is perceived to be a crooked race.

Punters fail to understand that bookmakers want straight racing! The Art of Bookmaking is all about drawing a profit from a balanced book, pure and simple. Punters only moan when they are not part of a supposed coup that might have been landed from time to time. Do you suppose that the bookmaker knew what was going on when those gambles were landed?

Why would the layer have accepted the bets given the coup in question, if they knew what was occurring? A bookmaker can back their judgement in laying prices when racing conditions are constant, which is preferable to the gamble that ensues when pricing up races when the going has changed dramatically.

Racegoers moan when outsiders invariably run well in such circumstances but who is forcing the punters to bet?

The bookmakers react to conditions as the Ring Inspector demands but the layers are betting in the dark in such circumstances, just as their potential clients are. When going racing or having a bet on the flat, look at the draw scenario first and foremost (taking changing ground into account) and bet accordingly, whichever side of the counter or exchanges you are playing from.

Basic Draw Details	
Ascot	Difficult to assess until the new course is utilised
Ayr	The sprint races are unpredictable but low numbers tend to have an advantage over seven furlongs and a mile.
Bath	High number are best, particularly when the ground is riding fast and horses run tight to the far rail. The slight elbow a furlong from home helps the leaders to remain in front.
Beverley	One of the most biased tracks in the country with high numbers dominating races over five furlongs. Horses over any distance hold an advantage when getting out fast and staying close to the rail.
Brighton	Low numbers tend to do best at Brighton, unless soft going prevails when it is best to keep a watching brief, with your money remaining firmly in your wallet.
Carlisle	High on firm, low on soft and stay in the bar at anything in between.
Catterick	Low numbers hold a slight advantage over the sprint trip.

Chepstow	High numbers hold an advantage but you need to be desperate for a bet to stake a wager on the level at the Welsh venue. I class this as a bookmaker's venue given the flat racing code.
Chester	The tight left hand bend two furlongs from the finish ensures that you need a low draw. The shorter the trip, the better the advantage.
Doncaster	Out of action until 2007.
Epsom	A high draw tends to be preferable over the flying five. Your selection(s) need to trap fast however, as horses can become hemmed in two furlongs from home with nowhere to go.
Folkestone	Either rail is the call over the minimum trip, whilst high numbers have the edge over six and seven furlongs.
Goodwood	Punters tend to focus on the sprint races but the real key is to be drawn high in races over seven furlongs and a mile.
Hamilton	Keep an eye on the Glasgow weather, as soft ground brings about an advantage for high numbers.
Haydock	Low numbers best on soft and heavy ground, conditions which occur on a regular basis at Haydock, even in the height of summer.
Kempton	How's your all-weather knowledge?
Leicester	Anything goes.
Lingfield	A draw near the stands side fence is preferable, especially when the number of runners mount up.
Musselburgh	Low over five furlongs, especially in yielding conditions.
Newbury	Get on and try not to lay the best horse, pure and simple.

Newcastle	Impossible. The field generally splits into two groups and I resent having to play guessing games regarding the best side of the track. The same can be said for other venues but at least decent racing is on the menu at those other courses. Lay on the round course by all means.
Newmarket (Rowley Mile)	The stands side rail tends to claim more than its fair share of successes.
Newmarket (July course)	Slow conditions do not prevail very often but low numbers hold the call in such circumstances.
Nottingham	Wouldn't have a bet at the track personally. Bad racing, bad venue, bad taste. I'm always listening to the vibes however, because I have yet to reach a position where I can ignore a quick buck!
Pontefract	A high draw comes into its own on poor ground.
Redcar	The Cleveland venue produces plenty of soft ground, when a high draw is usually preferable.
Ripon	High numbers do best on the round course, whilst it's something of a lottery which is the best rail in sprint races.
Salisbury	Well known for its changing policy by jockeys on days when the going alters from fast to slow. High numbers (far side) are preferred on fast ground, whilst low numbers have the edge when the horses track over to the stands side given soft or heavy conditions.
Sandown	High numbers are preferred on the straight track when plenty of runners are involved.

Thirsk	Low numbers over the far side have been known to dominate races, unless small fields are the order of the day.
Warwick	Low numbers hold a distinct advantage over the seven furlong trip.
Windsor	High numbers hold a tremendous advantage on the straight course when the ground is fast, especially in maiden events. Low numbers come into their own on slow ground.
Yarmouth	I do like to be beside the seaside but not from a racing perspective. The relevant Newmarket raiders from top yards are invariably more important than the draw.
York	The best horse usually wins, though low numbers (if any) marginally hold the call.

A similar scenario relates to ground conditions under the National Hunt code of racing.

The current season 2005/6 has been a poor one for the much-maligned Clerk of the Course up and down the land. To be truthful, the negative comments have been a long time in coming, as trainers have tried to understand the difficult position of the Clerk of the Course. Even Sandown's Andrew Cooper called it wrong on Ladbroke Hurdle day in January, when he declared that the going 'should be about the same as was the case on Boxing Day', which was basically good, good to soft in places with a few soft patches down the far side. Within hours, Mick Fitzgerald was telling Channel Four viewers that the going on the hurdles course (particularly) was desperate, with many horses failing to get home.

A similar scenario occurred at Taunton a couple of days later this year, when the going was described as good. The general opinion expressed by the professionals concerned was that it was an accurate assessment of the ground, yet the results suggested that the going was far more testing, with three winners hailing from Roselier stock, who invariably like plenty of give underfoot.

This is just another example of how much work is required if you are to take the sport seriously, either as a layer or a player. The Taunton example also reminds us of a previous statement in this publication, that 'one see is worth a thousand hears!'

National Hunt racecourses:	
Aintree	(Mildmay course): Flat and sharp. Left-handed. (Grand National course): Flat, galloping course. Left-handed.
Ascot	A testing circuit which should not change after the alterations come into place. Left-handed.
Ayr	A flat track with a run-in of 240 yards after the final fence. One and a half mile circuit. Left-handed.
Bangor	Flat (L/H) track for the nippy type.
Carlisle	Testing right-handed track with undulations. A dour test when the going is heavy.
Cartmel	An easy (parkland) left-handed course that suits flat horse types.
Catterick	An undulating and sharp left-hander.
Cheltenham	Generally testing, though much easier after impressive drainage work. Left-handed.
Chepstow	A really testing left-handed track that takes no prisoners.
Doncaster	Being redeveloped.

Exeter	A testing right-handed track that has severe uphill gradients.
Fakenham	Sharp left-handed track, easy to get home.
Folkestone	Easy fences on an undulating right-hand circuit.
Fontwell	(hurdles) Oval circuit, where pace injection down the far side is the order of the day. (steeplechase track): One of only two figure of eight circuits; suits course winners.
Haydock	Testing flat left-handed circuit with stiff fences, some with a drop landing.
Hereford	Unusual, almost square circuit with stiffish fences.
Hexham	Left-handed track with stiff finish but easy fences.
Huntingdon	Flat galloping right-handed circuit. Not too many horses come from off the pace to win.
Kelso	Half a mile run-in on the steeplechase circuit. A race is never over at Kelso until the judge calls the result!
Kempton	NH racing will take place on the old flat circuit.
Leicester	Undulating right-handed circuit, tough fencing circuit for novices.
Lingfield	Steep downhill track to negotiate three quarters of a mile from home. Suits a nippy type of horse.
Ludlow	A right-handed straightforward racecourse.
Market Rasen	Known also for its summer meetings nowadays.
Musselburgh	A flat sharp track with the emphasis on speed.

Newbury	One of the fairest courses in the land. Not too stiff, accommodating firm but fair fences.
Newcastle	An undulating stiff track that serves the winter code of racing best.
Newton Abbot	Flat and sharp right-handed course that makes little demand on the thoroughbred.
Perth	The spring meeting stands out as offering the best sport at the venue.
Plumpton	John Francome once reported the ground conditions here as either road-like or a mudbath and very rarely anything in between.
Sandown	A stiff galloping track, where the fairly ordinary looking railway fences sort out the men from the boys.
Sedgefield	Undulating left-handed track with straightforward fences.
Southwell	The famous venue where Tony McCoy remounted to win at exchange odds of 999/1. The scenario is the only reason for its fame.
Stratford	Left-handed track that makes few demands.
Taunton	Basic right-handed track.
Towcester	If your horse can get home here, it's okay anywhere.
Uttoxeter	A flat and galloping track that seems to get more than its fair share of rain.
Warwick	An undulating sharp track.
Wetherby	Going tends to get very tacky and horses struggle to last home on occasions.
Wincanton	Speedy types are suited to this right-handed venue.
Worcester	Flat galloping circuit for summer picnic clients.

Remember the old adage of horses for courses, which applies more to the jumping game than its flat counterpart.

Course winners, particularly course and distance winners should invariably be kept on the right side, whether you are a player or a layer.

Unless horses are trained by the top handlers, I'm inclined to oppose penalised horses at the start of their respective careers.

Two-year-olds on the flat and novice hurdlers with winning form tend to offer poor value for money, especially from a win perspective, though many of these young horses can be included as bankers in toteplacepot permutations. I also tend to lay horses that have run well on their debut (without having won) that are offered as short-priced favourites to make amends next time out. Until a horse has actually won, I'm inclined to take the beast on.

This attitude slightly contradicts my comments on penalised winners, which I must explain. These winners can be backed in my view but only if they are trained by any of the top handlers in the country. If the winners hail from smaller stables, I am inclined to take them on. The top trainers will have left something to work on in all probability and, with the more expensive young horses at their disposal, handlers realise that there is plenty of scope for improvement when they first send them racing.

This is often not the case with a smaller stable and the animal in question often represents poor value for money in my opinion. There are exceptions to the rule obviously, whilst I also appreciate that you are entitled to have your views on the subject.

Bookmakers (potential layers) have to use a rule of thumb where possible, otherwise they simply become punters, albeit from the other side of the counter or hod. As a stats anorak, I also take account of the figures that are generated on a daily basis.

Some people believe that stats are mere tools that anoraks use to organise their laying or backing of horses. I wouldn't disagree with that viewpoint but why not take advantage of the help that is available?

I made the point earlier about Mister McGoldrick and his Wetherby record, whilst it should be noted that the mighty Desert Orchid scored twenty-five of his twenty-seven victories on right-handed tracks. Twenty-three of those successes were gained at just four racecourses: Sandown, Wincanton, Kempton and Ascot. Do you think the victories in question were merely coincidental?

Juveniles present a lot of problems to punters and bookmakers and if you are like me, you will welcome any help that is on offer. So I thought it might aid layers and backers alike to list down the two-year-old records for the top ten English trainers, through money-earnings, last year.

The trainers are listed in order of their percentage achievements for the 2005 season:

Total Winners Compared to Runners		
Saeed Bin Suroor	35/156	22.4%
Mark Johnston	51/260	19.6%
Michael Stoute	21/116	18.1%
John Gosden	24/139	17.3%
Barry Hills	27/184	14.7%
Mick Channon	54/387	13.9%
Richard Hannon	60/446	13.4%
Brian Meehan	19/171	11.1%
Michael Jarvis	10/98	10.2%
Michael Bell	5/91	5.5%

First Time Out Winners		
Mark Johnston	15/80	18.7%
Saeed Bin Suroor	12/72	16.7%
Michael Stoute	8/57	14.0%
Mick Channon	10/79	12.6%
John Gosden	6/55	10.9%
Michael Jarvis	4/44	9.1%
Barry Hills	5/66	7.6%
Richard Hannon	6/97	6.2%
Brian Meehan	3/49	6.1%
Michael Bell	0/31	

Subsequent Outings (Winners from any subsequent 2-y-o runs)		
Saeed Bin Suroor	23/84	27.4%
Michael Stoute	13/59	22.0%
John Gosden	18/84	21.4%
Mark Johnston	36/180	20.0%

Barry Hills	22/118	18.6%
Richard Hannon	54/39	15.5%
Mick Channon	44/308	14.3%
Brian Meehan	16/122	13.1%
Michael Jarvis	6/54	11.1%
Michael Bell	5/60	8.3%

With only five figures topping the 20% mark, it's worth noting that four of those positive returns were achieved by trainers with subsequent runners (second and other runs of the season). If you glean nothing else from the stats, you should at least appreciate that backing Michael Bell's newcomers was the quick route to the workhouse!

The stats are not necessarily going to be repeated again in the 2006 campaign but the advice is to keep an eye on the progression of the relevant horses and trainers and if patterns emerge, you should keep on the right side of the findings.

Richard Hannon saddled three winners (including a 7/1 chance) and a 12/1 runner up in four of the opening two-year-old races at Windsor last year and, once again, if you chose to ignore that statistic, you landed up on the wrong side of the fence.

Richard saddled ten winners from forty-four juvenile raiders at Windsor last year and you ignore the trainer at the Berkshire venue at your peril, particularly in the two-year-old sector.

Mick Channon is the other trainer that churns out the two-year-old runners on a daily basis and it's worth noting that Mick's runners north of the border at Musselburgh and Hamilton yielded positive figures of 5/15 in 2005.

Barry Hills is famous for his sorties at Chester and it's

worth noting that three of his juvenile successes were gained at the venue with just six raiders in 2005. Furthermore, Barry boasts a 13/24 (54.2%) record from his two-year-old runners at Chester during the last five years.

I'll end the two-year-old sector by offering 2005 stats for the same trainers relating to nursery races (two-year-old handicaps), which are contested from July through to the end of the season.

Michael Stoute	2/9	(22.2%)
Saeed Bin Suroor	2/11	(18.2%)
Michael Jarvis	9/87	(14.3%)
Mark Johnston	5/45	(11.1%)
John Gosden	1/9	(11.1%)
Mick Channon	9/87	(10.3%)
Richard Hannon	7/71	(9.8%)
Brian Meehan	1/20	(5.0%)
Barry Hills	0/14	
Michael Bell	0/15	

The final three figures (1/49 for Meehan, Hills and Bell) should convince you to keep an eye on the stats throughout the season.

I do not put as much emphasis on breeding as I should in all probability but, when I find the time, I am amazed at some of the things I discover. What is the first thing you look for in your quest to find Classic winners for example?

The trainer's record in the race, the bare form lines, the projected going perhaps? Have a look at these facts and see if you are willing to start changing your habits:

The name of Northern Dancer is familiar to most of you

I'm sure but I did not realise that the great sire has featured in the breeding lines of:

Five of the last six Derby winners
Eight of the last nine 2,000 Guineas scorers
Four of the last six 1,000 Guineas winners
Four of the last six Oaks heroines
Four of the last five St Leger winners, whilst his son Nijinsky is the only colt to have won the Triple Crown since 1935!

If you want to ignore stats like that, I am not willing to join you!

I could go on to list several top class sires now but I'll just offer the name of Danehill and let you make up your own mind if you want to let breeding influence your betting.

Danehill (1986) By Danzig (Northern Dancer)

Jeremy Tree's outstanding sire ran in nine events, winning four times, was placed in two more and finished out of the money on just two occasions.

Career highlights: Finished third in the 2,000 Guineas behind Nashwan when beaten a length and a half by Dick Hern's champion. Danehill finished a neck in front of Markofdistinction that day and the Luca Cumani's Known Fact colt went on to lift the Queen Elizabeth II Stakes, Royal Ascot's 'Queen Anne,' along with Sandown's Trusthouse Forte Mile.

Danehill won the Group One Ladbroke's Sprint Cup at Haydock, beating Cricket Ball by two lengths on good to soft going as a three-year-old. Jeremy Tree's raider claimed the Group Three Cork & Orrery Stakes at Royal Ascot when defeating Nabeel Dancer by three lengths on firm ground.

His other victory at three years of age (did not race beyond 1989) was when shouldering 9-1 to victory in Newmarket's Free Handicap. Danehill was contesting Group One races in four of his five defeats, having been beaten first time up in a maiden event.

The Danzig colt contested races on good or faster ground seven times, winning three times and claiming place prize money on the other two occasions. Danehill won one of his two races on slower ground, being placed in the other event.

Distance details:
6 furlongs: Ran 5: won 3: placed 2
7 furlongs: Ran 2: won 1: unplaced 1
8 furlongs: Ran 2: placed 1: unplaced 1

Danehill sired the following brilliant performers: Banks Hill – Mozart – North Light – Rock Of Gibraltar and Westerner, among others. George Washington is the latest star to represent Danehill to devastating effect.

Danehill's sire Danzig (1977) was an outstanding stallion, responsible for no less that 47 worldwide Group One winners at the start of the 2005 season, including Dayjur, Mujahid and Burooj. The impressive part of the story, when reflecting how you might let these facts influence your laying and backing in the years to come, is that Danehill acted on all types of going, which not many horses achieve in top class events.

From a punting point of view, my advice would be to treat all bets like a bookmaker. Be greedy when the need arises and treat every race as a clean sheet of paper. Punters are far too flippant about the bets that they have staked in general. Many people stake a yankee bet, without even realising that the first runner is carrying seven bets of their outlay!

Horse 'A' is accountable for the accumulator, three of the doubles and three of the trebles and from a bookmaker's perspective, the bet is dead and buried in terms of its danger to the layer if the first horse is beaten.

As a settler in a busy shop, I would keep three piles of bets. I used to work in the Mecca shop in the Edgware Road in London, which was one of the busiest betting shops in the country. On a weekday, Mecca employed four cashiers, a pay-out person and two settlers, aside from the manager!

The three piles of bets were divided into race by race business, speculative bets that had not started in terms of race times and those that had a loser included in the relevant wagers. As soon as a loser featured in a yankee bet it was discarded into the also ran pile and, whilst I would work through those wagers when the time allowed, priority had to be given to the other two piles of bets.

The race by race pile was important, as the company held the view that the sooner a client was paid out on a winning bet, the quicker they might reinvest the winnings. The second pile was important because of the fact that all opportunities for the client to win still remained. This is the point I am trying to get across about taking the bookmaker's perspective when placing a bet.

When a punter has secured a trio of winners with their three opening selections, the general feeling (I assure you) is that they have more than achieved their original aim.

The importance of the fourth selection is invariably lost on them but the bookmaker is oh so aware about the difference between three and four winners on a betting slip.

Three winners in a yankee wager equates to four winning bets and, if the last selection is beaten, seven bets have been lost. Most punters do not appreciate the significance of that final fourth selection in those circumstances.

Under no circumstances should you bring previous bets on horses into the equation. Do not become swayed to support or oppose a horse simply because you backed or layed it last time out, either as a player or a layer. The race in question is a unique event and should be treated as such. Horses on the upgrade should always be treated with respect, no matter how high the handicapper has raised the horse, or if a trainer has delusions of grandeur relating to the task in question. The percentages of horses that actually win a race is small and all scorers should be respected.

Some bookmakers and punters attach a dreaded (Timeform) squiggle against a horse, believing it to be ungenuine, possibly having its own thoughts about the game. This move is acceptable, providing the person involved is consistent with their methods and is willing to remove the horse in question should a change of performance occur.

A leopard very rarely changes it spots but a closed mind is a negative mind, that can become very costly!

CHAPTER 5

Greyhound Racing

This is the sector of the business that has basically fallen apart at the seams and most of the problems can be equated to the greed of the bookmaker. There are too many races covered in the shops now and that comment governs both horse and greyhound racing.

Coupled with real racing, there are also the virtual events to take into account, apart from the lottery style ball games which are encouraged in licensed premises.

I don't like to harp on about the old days but betting shops were never busier, in midweek, than when there was half decent racing from two meetings on the quarter and half hour mark, that fitted in conveniently with one dog programme which kept clients happy.

Saturday mornings were geared towards an eleven o'clock start at Hackney and the forecast double bets would start piling up on the settler's desk from the minute the shops opened their doors to eager punters.

I worked in West London shops in those days and the norm would be to expect the thick end of one hundred slips of forecast doubles and such before the hare approached the traps for the first time.

No, it wasn't all good news for the bookmakers in those

halcyon days, because if one of the early events on those eight race cards produced a half decent forecast of traps one to two or six to five, the alarm bells would start ringing and the telephone lines to head office were red hot.

Anything up to a third of those morning bets would have those trap numbers included in the wagers and it's not too much of an exaggeration to suggest that Saturday's business in those days could, on occasions, be dependent on the outcome of the eight Hackney events. Too many one and twos or six and fives and bookmakers were on their heels trying to recover the loss, as horse racing took over centre stage shortly after one o'clock.

If the results had gone well however, the layers were well on their way to a good day and, although lunch was never on the agenda for shop staff on this busiest day of the week, everybody could digest a hastily eaten sandwich that much easier if middle trap runners had performed well that morning.

What happened to this potentially lucrative business?

Bookmakers became greedy, as initially the number of races were increased from eight to ten and then from ten to twelve soon afterwards. Some greyhound meetings now accommodate fourteen races on the BAGS circuit! The number of straight forecast doubles for eight races in the early days was twenty-eight, which extended to one hundred and twelve bets if punters wanted to go for it by wagering reversed trap numbers. The equivalent number of bets for twelve races is sixty-six (and two hundred and sixty-four reversed), which the punters just about coped with, even if greyhound supporters had to reduce their unit stake to accommodate one of their favourite wagers.

The extended number of races also affected the shop

staff, because although time was always tight from the end of the Hackney meeting until the time of the first horse racing event, one of the staff could usually pop out to the bakers to collect the order on behalf of the whole team. With twelve races on the agenda, all that planning went out of the window, as greyhound and horse racing action were being staged at the same time, whereby there was barely time to put the kettle on for a cup of tea, let alone eat what could only be described as a pauper's lunch. The civilised running of a shop was thrown into chaos, the afternoon yankee bets were held up as other punters were trying to get their dog bets on.

The cashiers found it difficult to check their tills, to try and ensure that all the staff could make a hasty departure from the premises later in the afternoon, without the need to look for potentially lost money or differentials on the till rolls. If a mistake had been made in the first few hours of trading, it was far easier to find the error at lunchtime, rather than trawl through the whole day's business after the last race when everybody was exhausted.

The extended dog meetings were bad news all round and the manager's job and that of the staff was no longer an enjoyable exercise on a Saturday morning. But what did the bookmakers also concoct around that time do you suppose?

The powers that be introduced a second meeting (Crayford) on a Saturday morning and, not only did this destroy the goodwill of the shop staff but the move forced the punters into an impossible position with their morning wagers. Cast your mind back to the initial outlay I talked of and you will recall that punters invested heavily on either twenty-eight straight forecast doubles, or one hundred and twelve reverse forecast doubles.

Now the punter was being asked to consider accumulative units of double the sixty-six bets (Hackney and Crayford) and two times the two hundred and sixty-four units for reversed forecast wagers and the bookmakers couldn't understand why the forecast double business eventually collapsed! One dope of an area manager asked me why the Saturday morning business had collapsed on one occasion, failing to understand that a punter who had made a habit of backing trap one to beat trap two at Hackney, was now being asked to open his wallet to back the same numbers at Crayford.

The Area Manager didn't see that the punter was too afraid of backing their favourite numbers at one meeting and not the other, because as sure as sod's law exists, they knew what would happen!

This is, of course, exactly what happened with the national lottery, as an unsuspecting public began to invest in their birthday numbers, without the realisation that millions of customers would be duty bound to make the same investment week upon week.

And what do you suppose was the next move on a Saturday night?

Just like the bookmakers, the regulators allowed a second draw to be made and potential investors were once again forced into a corner, fearing that they would miss out on a big win. What has happened since with the national lottery - scratch cards etc. - is nothing short of a scandal and the cynics who initially suggested that the original idea was a 'tax on the poor' have been proved right. It's all well and good that the liberal types scream that it is a matter of choice for the public but since when have Joe Soap and his pals been able to make sensible decisions?

And whilst I'm on the subject, why can sixteen and seventeen-year-olds play the national lottery but cannot walk into a betting shop, let alone stake a wager? Don't give me the charity answers please because, just like the businessmen and women who made the decisions to add on the extra dog races and meetings, the real money is going to line the pockets of those who are already wealthy enough.

On a lighter note however (though not for the bookmakers), I'm going to let you in on a major mistake the layers made many years ago. Tricasts on greyhound races had just been introduced on 'Open' races on the BAGS (Bookmakers Afternoon Greyhound Service) and, as always in these instances, Joe Soap and his mates were looking for ways to make the most out of the new wager, if such an opportunity occurred. Sure enough, the bookmakers had failed to see what was coming next when the layers made an elementary mistake.

Forecast returns are basically governed by an add a point method.

As a rule of thumb guide and using starting prices of the first two dogs home (as an example) being 2/1 and 7/1, the forecast would pay around the £16.00 mark (to a one pound investment).

The add a point scenario applies to the price of the second greyhound in question; hence 2 x 8 = 16.

When the tricast was introduced for the BAGS service, the bookmakers made a blunder by multiplying the forecast dividend by the price of the third greyhound to finish; hence the example I offered in the previous sentence might have paid £48.00 (16 x 3) if the third greyhound had been returned at 3/1. The point they missed was that the price of the greyhound in question could not have been 3/1 in real terms, because there were only four dogs left (after the first and second had been established) that could fill the position.

Joe Soap and his merry men went into action, though on this occasion, by way of a change, they acted in exemplary fashion.

These merry men searched for a Robin Hood style leader that they could use on the inside and, as is always the case where money is concerned, they didn't have to wait long for the guv'nor to emerge.

The lads wanted a bookmaker who stood at a track to move the market in their favour and that is exactly what happened.

Having chosen their venue carefully, where plenty of 'Open' action was to be found, the bookmakers job was to knock out the price of dogs that were deemed not good enough to win the respective races but were more than capable of finishing third.

I stood in the shops and watched greyhounds drifting from 5/1 to 10/1 with a smile on my face, knowing what was going on.

It didn't take much money to force prices down in those days and the bookmaker in question went about tipping up the front two in the market the previous night and all through the day, using the usual whisper method, knowing that the two dogs in question were going to be backed off the boards when the betting opened up. This resulted in bookmakers at the track extending the prices of the no-hopers... led by Robin himself! Greyhounds that might have been expected to start at 6/1 and 8/1 were drifting out to 12's and 14's respectively, bumping up the potential tricast dividend.

The form students among the scallywags decided which greyhounds they were going to class as third best, bearing in mind that a full cover scenario for a greyhound (a certain trap number to finish third to any other two dogs in the field) would require an investment of twenty bets. I believe the gang usually gambled on two greyhounds (forty bets), praying that one of those dogs would finish third.

The sting wasn't perfect by any means, because the said greyhound(s) still had to finish third for the bet to be successful but a lot of money was won before the bookmakers cottoned on to what was going on, which took longer than you might imagine.

Back to basics now however, by asking bookmakers how they could revive fortunes in this division of the betting sector?

The forecast doubles scenario is dead and buried now unfortunately and no percentage of the marketing budget can retrieve the situation. Bookmakers don't seem to have filled the void however and, as a consequence, betting on greyhound racing is in decline. It strikes me that bookmakers should offer an incentive to customers to retain their interest between events on the horse racing front.

A marketing plan I would use could be termed 'Next Trap Up', which would offer punters a realistic opportunity of increasing their return without additional stakes, with additional enjoyment in the race in question. Next trap up would apply to single bets during the BAGS meetings only, whereby punters place their win bets in the usual fashion (nothing more is asked of them – no complication) and the bet is settled in the same manner as usual, unless the next trap up finishes second.

If a client has placed a successful wager on trap two for example, an additional payment (perhaps 10% of winnings – not stake) would be added to their return if trap three finished second.

A further bonus could apply (maybe an additional 5%) if trap four finished third, the traps two and three sequence having been extended for the race to finish 2-3-4.

The additional payments would only be paid for six-dog races and, in the circumstances of trap six winning, trap one (and then trap two) would be deemed as the next trap(s) up. Similarly, trap numbers would have to read 5-6-1 for the additional 15% return to be added for a punter that has successfully backed trap five.

Bookmakers already know that the BAGS service is one of their better services in terms of potential profit margin, as the returned percentages on these races are often very high. It is commonplace for a BAGS race to open offering punters very little by way of value. A betting shop client will often witness percentages of around 40 % on the first show at a BAGS meeting and, if the layers chalked up similar prices at Walthamstow at an evening meeting, the bookmakers would be chased out of the stadium.

These prices offer the bookmakers an opportunity to give something back to the punter, which should result in positive PR between the company and its clients.

This idea is one that independent bookmakers could easily offer to clients, in their quest to fend off the big companies that trade just down the road. The margin (in percentages) for the potential bonus to be paid, ensures that independent bookmakers could accommodate such an incentive, even if the layer decides to implement a maximum wager that the offer applies to. That is the bookmaker's prerogative at all times.

I am not naïve enough to believe that a bookmaker should be offering such incentives to a one-off punter who walks into a shop, stakes a hundred pounds on a live greyhound, picks up the bonus and is never seen again. Next trap up is all about accommodating regular clients.

One of my ideas was utilised within the industry many years ago, when the 'Greyhound Placer' was established in the William Hill shops. I took the idea to Mike Palmer who was the Greyhound Editor at the Racing Post back in 1995 and the rest is history as they say.

Unlike the toteplacepot which is a wager governed by a pool, I established the bet would be based on the starting price returns of the greyhounds and then process the returned result using a sliding scale of points. The points would be multiplied race on race for the six races until a dividend was declared. The bet has not exactly taken off as I would have liked and perhaps it's time for an injection of invention in the greyhound sector, though next time up at least offers the public something for nothing, which is more than punters are getting now. The success or failure of many of the actual greyhound stadiums is now dependent on how many restaurant customers they can lure to the venue.

Just as the horse racing venues have been buoyed by the number of corporate clients they host, greyhound stadiums now cater for a different type of client, especially when compared to Stan Bowles and his chums down at the White City on Thursday and Saturday nights back in the seventies. Many of these restaurant clients (respectfully) don't know one end of a greyhound from another and I'm surprised the industry as a whole has not catered for the new punters. The colour of greyhound racing is of one the sport's attractions from my viewpoint, though the sand that has replaced the lush green turf has detracted from the spectacle to a degree.

I was watching the clients in a restaurant recently, all trying to establish their bets, with the tote collector anxiously trying to determine what was required from each individual punter.

It struck me that there should be a pile of betting slips on the tables when guests arrive, which would add colour and logic to proceedings. These slips would have self explanatory rules on the reverse side to explain tote betting in more detail than is currently in operation, whilst the colourful (red-blue-white-back-orange-stripes) front side of the coupon would house the options open to the punters in mark sense form, identical to the national lottery format. This would lead to less mistakes being made on behalf of both the tote operators and the public, whilst slips could be retained as evidence of proof of the client's intention, though the onus on the punter to check their tote tickets would still be in place.

Perhaps one greyhound placer on the card could be made available for a tote pool between races five and ten, not too early to miss clients who were late on parade but finishing well before the last race, not to deter potential investors who want to leave to beat the traffic, or those that need to return home before their child has had a chance to abuse the babysitter.

I believe it was either Park Royal or Hendon that last paid out on three places at a greyhound stadium through the tote and I'm wondering if the on-course greyhound placer could offer this additional incentive for potential investors. The likely players of this particular bet are not essentially seeking great rewards from my viewpoint, more an interest that offers them a realistic chance of some extended activity in a pool bet for a relatively small outlay. I would be surprised if such a client was unwilling to part with two pounds per unit for such entertainment.

Printed A4 marketing flyers could adorn every table explaining the greyhound placer, depicting recent dividends where positive declarations had been in evidence at recent meetings.

CHAPTER 6

Football

As many readers will know, I write a daily column for sportinglife.com and people still suggest that the dear old Queen Mother's favourite newspaper was the best racing journal, although it ceased to trade as a printed publication back in May 1998.

Punters still complain about the spread of form over several pages of the tabloid *Racing Post* publication though, equally, anyone who tried to cope with the Life on a windy day at Newmarket would suggest that the smaller newspaper was definitely the right decision to take! What cannot be argued however, is the way that the *Racing Post* has improved its sports coverage, promoting sports betting to an unprecendented level, highlighted by its football columns. Some companies now report that as much as 50% of their business is created from the football sector.

The World Cup Finals attracted a frenzy of betting and bookmakers up and down the land targeted punters to get more than their fair share of the market. What bookmakers should have done however was to invent new ways of luring the punters into their own particular den of iniquity, in order to make the most of a competition nationally advertised on their behalf. There are several new markets to attract punters to the shops, such as Asian handicaps and further opportunities for different wagers on the Internet but more still needs to be achieved in order to attract the occasional punter.

The young business types would be one of my personal targets, those that don't know an offside decision from an indirect free kick but love the thrill of the chase anyway. I would have established a market for them that is perceived to offer an even money chance, possibly advertising the bets in unusual publications such as the *Financial Times* and City AM. This type of basic bet might appeal to the City slickers:

How many goals will be scored in 90 minutes between Germany and Costa Rica in the opening game of the championships?

Offering 5/6 an odd number of goals and 5/6 an even result (includes the 0-0 scoreline), punters would have an interest right through to the final whistle and with this type of potential investor, a return of 84% over a two hour period is tantamount to winning the pools!

This type of player is happy to secure a 2% return on a weekly investment, so anything approaching even money would be very well received, whilst the PR of successful bets for the punter would be beneficial to the losing bookmakers beyond their wildest dreams. Sometimes the bookmaker should act like this potential new brand of punter, whereby a fall leads to eventual profit from a dusting down of oneself, by working harder to recover losses and adopting an obsession to turn red type into black.

City types eat PMA (positive mental attitude) for breakfast and if you, as a bookmaker, can tune in to their frequency, you could discover untapped potential that has been bubbling under the surface for many years.

Profit margin is of course important but a profit of 5% from total turnover of £5 million is infinitely preferable to a surplus of 7% from half the stakes. Here's a bet I thought of fully twenty years ago, though punters reading this book will have to excuse my standing on the side of the bookmaker during the explanation. Imagine two other World Cup matches this year that are being played on the same day, holding no real interest outside of making money.

Let's take the matches which were played in Group C on 11 June as an example. Mexico met Iran whilst Portugal took on Angola.

Just for this example, let's be generous as far as the favourites are concerned by offering 2/5 Mexico and 1/4 Portugal.

What are you, as bookmakers, going to offer on these games?

The usual correct score options, alongside half time/full time betting and perhaps the last goalscorer as well as the first?

And of course there is always the double that punters can latch onto, which at 2/5 and 1/4 evaluates to a return of £1.75 (just over 8/11) for every pound invested. A return nonetheless, which is not going to inspire your potential clients, though the double is the clue you should be seeking in the quest to obtain your share of the market. Instead of offering the tired old odds of 2/5 Mexico and 1/4 Portugal, wouldn't the following example offer more interest to the prospective client?

3/1 PORTUGAL
4/1 THE DRAW
9/2 MEXICO

Okay, I hear you say, it looks different, the bet offers an interest by coupling the two matches but where is my profit margin and what's the draw scenario? As turf accountants, bookmakers always have to be fed the bottom line first, so essentially I am assuring you (as the layer) of a potentially higher profit margin than laying individual odds of the two teams (2/5 & 1/4), whilst making the wager look more attractive at one and the same time.

Focusing on the price of the double (8/11 – thereabouts), you add another 10% to your potential profit line by working this bet to a percentage figure of 63.6, which is evaluated by adding 10% (5.8) to the 57.9% figure we know that odds of 8/11 equate to.

The bet is marketed thus:

Which team will win by the largest number of goals?

3/1 PORTUGAL
4/1 THE DRAW
9/2 MEXICO

So how do you determine the prices?

Return to the price of the double (8/11) and multiply the return (£1.72) by the price which you think best describes the chance of the teams both winning by the same margin (i.e. a "draw"), which might be 7/4 (£2.75) in your opinion.

Evaluate the return that should give you a figure of £4.73 or 3.73/1.

Bearing in mind that punters rarely sit on the fence (opt

for the draw), I've offered 4/1 for this scenario.

How do you now evaluate the prices of the two teams to "win"?

Subtract the percentage figure of the draw (20.0%) from the extended profit margin of 63.6% and you should find an outstanding percentage now available of 43.6%.

Bearing in mind that Portugal were the shortest price of the two teams to win, logic suggests (though homework is required re the scoring/conceding of goals relating to all four countries) that Portugal should be favourites to win this match. I have split the available percentage up by offering 3/1 Portugal (25.0%) and 9/2 Mexico (18.2%) which, coupled with the draw offers combined percentages of 63.2%.

Whilst offering the punter a unique wager, which offers them potential interest of 180 minutes play, I have increased your potential profit margin by 5.3%, an increase of 9.2% on the original figure.

Have you detected the real coup here yet?

The bet is governed that both teams have to win their respective matches... or all stakes are lost. Look at what we have achieved.

We are enticing the punter to play for a novelty bet that offers the client a more interesting wager. We have increased our potential profit margin by 5.3% (9.2%). Both teams have to win or the bookmaker swags all the cash and, even if Portugal and Mexico both triumph, the punter must still decide which scenario they will opt for.

The Art of Bookmaking is to attract clients to bet, whilst increasing your potential profit, as well as your turnover! As suggested earlier in this chapter however, turnover is the essential ingredient to bookmaking. Yes, bookmakers have to make a living but without turnover there is no profit whatsoever.

In this example we have potentially created increased turnover and profit but even if both Portugal and Mexico have won, coupled with your potential client selecting the right option, think of all the positive PR you will receive.

I compiled the type of prices offered on behalf of the bookmakers in that last example, so it's only fair if I balance the books by offering punters this advice, as written for the readers of the *Inside Edge* magazine last year:

'Don't be fooled by those wily bookies! Given half a chance they'll trick you into placing football bets you haven't even heard of, let alone want to bet on.'

It wasn't long ago that bookies were legally banned from enticing punters into shops with window advertisements. The layers couldn't even play a radio in the shop in case it encouraged people to dance! Strange but true. Anything goes these days – which is dangerous for punters as it means the bookies have ample opportunity to tempt you into bets that are a complete waste of time. They're only offering sweets these days because competition is so fierce. That's why there are so many unusual and deeply unprofitable (for the player) bets out there on every street corner and betting website.

Most betting adverts are for football markets – young people seem less interested in horse racing and more interested in football, so bookies try to lure punters into the shop on a diet of banner headlines and football prices. But which are the most dangerous bets for punters to play? I have come up with a list of five footy wagers that smart punters will avoid – follow suit and your betting bank balance will look a lot healthier!

1. First Goal scorer

This scenario isn't as bad as it used to be because of all the team line-up news presented by the media – which at least gives you a clearer indication of which players will be on the pitch when the game kicks off. If you have to place a bet in this sector, however, only do so when the teams have been confirmed an hour before the match in question. Unclaimed betting slips up and down the land as a result of non-runners in the first goal scorer sector would fill a recycling tank on an annual basis.

Even if you do bet just before kick-off, the percentages are stacked against you as prices have been compiled several days in advance of the match. Unlike punters, bookies will never take a chance and the odds on offer confirm the fact this is a bad market to play. How do you predict who will be the first player to find the net? What are the factors to bear in mind? Even though certain players (strikers) are likely to net more than their share of first goals, it's impossible to select a player with any degree of confidence.

Layers will be wise to players in form and price up the forwards accordingly. The only area where you might score the occasional hit is with dead-ball strikes from lesser-known players at the likes of Wigan, Sunderland and Birmingham City. The bookies may be unaware of all the free-kick specialists at such clubs but does this slight glimmer of hope render a first goal scorer bet as good value for the potential investor?

The answer has to be no.

Consider how many ways there are for a team to score a first goal. Remember the fact that you are hoping the opposition haven't already scored and you'll see that there are too many uncertainties to play this wager seriously.

2. Last Goal scorer

The bookies dreamed up this nice little earner – for them, not you – a few years ago and many of the rules explained in the first goal scorer bet also apply here.

The starting line-up isn't so important, as different players will be on the pitch at the end because of substitutions. This makes the bet even more difficult to call – how do you know which players the coach will bring off, will be sent on from the bench, or might get injured during the game?

If you must play this wager, consider defenders first and foremost, because they at least represent some sort of value for money.

Whilst defenders tend to go forward for corners and free kicks throughout a match, this will happen more often as the game approaches its final minutes, particularly if your selection is playing for the team that is losing. So if you have backed a defender whose team are trying to scramble back into the game, you at least get a fighting chance.

Strikers should be classed as non-runners, because they are substituted more often than defenders and their prices nearly always represent poor value.

Do you want to be on a 4/1 striker in the closing minutes, or a 33/1 defender? The defender has to be the call – but better still, ignore this market altogether.

3. Half Time/Full Time

You have to admire the downright aggression of

bookmakers, because in this bet the layers are asking you to name not one result but two! As if correctly predicting the outcome of a football match wasn't difficult enough, here you have to estimate which team will be ahead at half-time and at full-time. What adds insult to injury is that bookies potentially gain more profit by laying these bets, having already made your job twice as difficult in the process.

Taking average prices across the board, a team that is 6/4 to win a game actually becomes a 5/4 chance when adding up the percentages using the three options open to punters betting on the same team. To confirm this statement as true, simply add up the percentages of the three variables (losing at half-time, win at full-time; drawing at half-time, win at full-time; and winning at halftime, win at full-time).

The scenario becomes even worse for firmer favourites, as a team that is offered at 1/3 to win a match can be as short as 1/6 in this three-way scenario. The price for the win-win scenario is roughly 4/6, the draw-win is often priced up around 7/2, whilst 28/1 is on offer for a team to be behind at half-time but come through to win the game at 90 minutes.

The combined percentages add up to a price of 1/6, so ignore this sector for the health of your wallet.

4. Fixed-Odds Shirt Numbers

This is football bingo. Fixed-odds companies are offering punters bets on shirt numbers in the following format:

'Have a bet on tonight's match and if your player gets sent off, we'll refund you a pound for every figure on his back' – so, if a player wearing number seven is sent off, punters will receive seven to their account.

This is simply ridiculous. The bookies are just trying to trick you into placing a bet on tonight's game that you probably wouldn't have otherwise placed. Such wagers completely overlook basic betting principles of looking for value and studying the form-book or trends. It's a lottery - avoid it at all costs.

5. Sections Lists

A crooked smile twists across my ageing face every time I look at this scenario. I smile because I simply cannot understand how punters keep falling for such a blindingly obvious trap created by the bookmakers. Punters are asked to predict the outcome of a minimum of one match out of six in each of five sections of matches, which are pre-determined by the bookmaker. You need all your selections to win and, based on the best prices available, the bookmakers will tell you to 'select one team from each section' for minimum odds of 13/2, two teams from each section for 68/1 and three teams from each section for 690/1.

Accumulators involving so many teams really are a complete and utter waste of money. I've lost count of the number of red lines I've crossed through these bets when I managed betting shops – the odds are stacked against you.

What really annoys me about punters who invest in this market, is the fact that they are compelled to bet on matches that they might otherwise have ignored. The layers have determined which matches fit into each section and the punter is controlled to consider the chosen games.

It's a bet devised by the bookmaker, so that automatically means it offers poor value.

As if to make matters worse, a lot of punters treat the bet as an afterthought – they place their normal weekend bets and then have a go at the section list bet for a bit of added value. Added value? They're pouring money down the drain. It's merely a marketing scam – so don't be fooled!

I'm honestly not trying to stop punters having a bit of fun (especially in World Cup year) but that's the only way you should interpret these wagers. If you have had a decent day and want to have some fun on a televised match that evening, spend a couple of quid on one of the markets if you must but please, just a couple of quid.

There are more football examples of potential new wagers further on in the book.

CHAPTER 7

Snooker, Golf and Cricket

Snooker

Snooker has taken something of a downturn in recent years, despite Ronnie O'Sullivan's brilliance and the controversy he has caused. Perhaps the sport has suffered from over-exposure in recent times, though the World Championship still seems as popular as ever. It will be interesting to see if moving the venue from the Crucible Theatre in Sheffield (in the offing I believe) will have a major effect on the competition, as snooker and Sheffield go together like golf and St Andrews from my standpoint.

Snooker is a good sport to focus on regarding the pricing up of tournaments, particularly from an ante-post perspective. This scenario is different from the sport of kings of course, because withdrawals generally do not occur; hence more realistic prices are on offer from the moment odds are chalked up. These prices were on offer (average prices across the board) for the 2005 World Championships on 10 April, a short time before the tournament started:

5/4 R. O'Sullivan
9/2 S. Hendry
9/1 M. Williams
10/1 J. Higgins
11/1 S. Maguire
16/1 P. Hunter
28/1 P. Ebdon
33/1 K. Doherty

The important point to note, is that by adding up the percentages on these front eight players, you will deduce that the bookmakers were already betting over round, which means that they have more than covered their potential 100% book on just these fancied players. With another twenty-four players on their side, how could bookmakers possibly lose on the tournament? The business isn't as simple as all that obviously but you must note that the layers always look to cover their 100% field with the realistic winners in any market, particularly covering the three sports highlighted in this chapter.

The horses for courses rules apply in snooker, as anyone who has laid Jimmy White (or Brown!) at Wembley will know to their cost. I was compiling the odds for a company at Wembley many years ago and quickly learned how popular Jimmy was at the venue!

Betting from year to year, bookmakers will have earned a profit by laying the popular cockney but it's a different ball game entirely from a round-by-round perspective. Jimmy has confounded pundits year on year by staging remarkable comebacks at the table when seemingly dead and buried and most of them to the delight of his colossal army of fans, particularly those from the London area.

On a side note for a moment, I should offer a true story, which serves as a warning that, no matter how clever we think we are, there is always somebody that knows more about any given situation.

I was in the betting booth at Wembley one year, having priced up the players to what I thought were the correct odds and there was little (if any) margin for punters to fleece this particular compiler, or so I thought! The legendary punter Harry Findlay was hovering around the cash register, which was nothing out of the ordinary and offered a bank roll of notes relating to two of the players in the tournament who were playing their respective matches that day (Tony Knowles and Tony Drago as I recall). He asked for the relevant (short) prices on offer, introducing a third option which just happened to be a nag in a novice hurdle race at Huntingdon.

Wanting to take the punter on, I was anxious to get the money in the hod, having deduced from the trade press that the horse in question was a 4/7 chance, which made the potential chunky treble no more than a 7/4 liability, with the two snooker players priced up at 2/5 and 1/4.

You might imagine the look on my face when the horse scored at 6/4, the potential treble now paying 9/2! You don't need me to add that Knowles and Drago both hosed in and the egg left on my face was still dripping into the till as I reeled off the notes to pay Harry who had turned over this rookie in some style.

The most popular bet in the sport of snooker involves correct frame betting, where odds are offered for both players to win by a certain margin. Punters might suppose that bookmakers fiddle about with the figures until they come up with what appear to be realistic prices but they would be a million miles away from the truth. It should be noted that these prices are mathematically biased, the same as the majority of other wagers in any betting market. To determine the prices you have to get back to basics by knowing your percentages and how the pairing of odds using two opposites are calculated.

In a two-runner scenario, be it horse racing, snooker or football (or any other situation), the accepted opposite price for one player that is priced at 4/7 is 5/4. This is the accepted margin for bookmakers to apply in a two-runner field. The full list is offered below, of which the majority hover around a potential 6 to 8% profit for bookmakers in their ideal world.

5/6 & 5/6 (total of 109.0%)
8/11 & Evs (total of 107.9%)
4/6 & 11/10 (total of 107.6%)
8/13 & 6/5 (total of 107.4%)
4/7 & 5/4 (total of 108.0%)
8/15 & 11/8 (total of 107.3%)
1/2 & 6/4 (total of 106.7%)
4/9 & 13/8 (total of 107.3%)
2/5 & 7/4 (total of 107.8%)
4/11 & 2/1 (total of 106.6%)
1/3 & 9/4 (total of 105.8%)
2/7 & 5/2 (total of 106.4%)
1/4 & 11/4 (total of 106.7%)
2/9 & 3/1 (total of 106.8%)
1/5 & 10/3 (total of 106.4%)
1/6 & 7/2 (total of 107.9%)

How do bookmakers price up frame betting between two

players?

The answer as always is by simple arithmetic. The layers rarely (if ever) price up a market without returning to their accountancy traditions.

Player 'A' is contesting a best of nine-frame match at Wembley against player 'B' in this first example. Player 'A' is a 1/3 chance to win, against odds of 9/4 for player 'B'. The two percentages equate to a book of 105.8%. We need that basic figure 105.8 to work from.

There are ten prices to offer (5-0 – 5-1 – 5-2 – 5-3 – 5-4 for each player), so let's adopt a stance where we are looking to bet to 120.9%.

We need to find the figure with which to multiply the basic odds (1/3 and 9/4) and this is the procedure. By dividing the required percentage figure of 120.9 by the original 105.8, we deduce that the multiplication figure in this instance is 1.142.

We now multiply the base percentages 75.0% (player 'A') and 30.8% (player 'B') by the 1.142 result, which now means that we can bet to 85.6% ('A') and 35.2% ('B').

The prices could now be offered along these lines:

A'	SETS	'B'
13/2	5-0	25/1
5/1	5-1	18/1
10/3	5-2	14/1
4/1	5-3	11/1
7/1	5-4	8/1
= 85.6%		= 35.2%

A similar scenario occurs in this second example, which is a first to ten match which could have been staged at The Crucible Theatre.

Player 'C' has been priced up at 2/5 to beat player 'D' who is on offer at 7/4. The percentages and the extended prices (in brackets) are as follows:

Player 'C': 71.4 multiplied by 1.214 equates to (86.6).
Player 'D': 36.4 multiplied by 1.214 equates to (44.2)

We are betting to higher percentages in this match, because we have more frames to price up. We opted for an over-round book of 130.9%. The point figure at the end of the percentages quoted can deviate a few fractions from time to time, as in this case. The multiplications evaluated to 130.9% in this instance. The original percentages equated to 107.8%, divided into the required 130.9 figure, which gave us our multiplication figure of 1.214.

'C'	SETS	'D'
50/1	10-0	250/1
33/1	10-1	200/1
16/1	10-2	100/1
11/1	10-3	66/1
8/1	10-4	33/1
13/2	10-5	22/1
6/1	10-6	16/1
15/2	10-7	12/1
10/1	10-8	10/1
12/1	10-9	8/1
= 86.4%		= 44.4%

In both examples, I have compiled the prices as I saw fit, without having characters to take into account.

In pricing up players like Ronnie O'Sullivan, as an example, there is more of a killer instinct in his style of play when he is on song and compilers might choose to reduce the price of the whitewash when Ronnie is competing in a match. I have suggested in the first example that the 1/3 favourite is likely to win by a scoreline of 5-2. The outsider of the two players would scramble home in the decider according to yours truly, if they were to prevail at all.

In the second example, the 2/5 favourite is likely to win 10-5 according to my book, with the outsider potentially squeezing home by the narrowest margin again.

In the first example, it should be noted that the warmer of the two favourites is expected to win by a margin nearer to a whitewash than to a final deciding frame. The second example, utilising the 2/5 favourite, suggests that the match will be marginally closer, right on the half way quota of frames.

Some compilers would have a sliding scale table at their disposal that they have prepared down the years. Using the second example again, a 1/2 favourite might be expected to win 10-7, compared to a 4/7 jolly who could be favoured to win 10-8 according to the frame betting using this sliding scale method. The actual prices quoted are the license that the compiler has in his armoury but only after basic mathematics have been applied.

The Art of Bookmaking is to work hard at compiling prices, not guessing at prices just because the percentages have been extended for the bookmaker's benefit. Take advantage of the figures that are in your (the bookmaker's) favour.

Golf

Golf has well and truly taken over as the third most popular sport for punters, if you combine horse and greyhound racing together and accept that football claims the number two position. The coverage by Sky Sports is second to none and, whereas a few short years ago we were confined to betting on the four major events in the main, punters can invest in tournaments on both sides of the Atlantic on a weekly basis. Tag on the Ryder Cup every other year and you have a recipe for success in one of the few sports left that is contested by decent individuals, which should be the case I guess, as golf professionals are probably the most envied of all sports men and women in the world today. Outside of tennis (too much like hard work) and cricket (too technical by far), where else can you be paid to follow the sun all around the world?

Prices for the 2005 Open were on offer 12 months ago and these were the general quotes:

11/4 T. Woods
7/1 E. Els
10/1 V. Singh
11/1 P. Mickleson

Heed the words written in the snooker example, when I suggested that bookmakers were intent to protect their margins by ensuring that popular and leading players would command at least 100% of the market. Bookmakers were betting the thick end of 8/11 that one of the big four was going to lift the Claret Jug, with more than one hundred other players to take into account, who were headed by

South Africa's Retief Goosen who was generally available at just 16/1, making the front five a collective price just short of 8/13.

Layers would argue that golf constitutes a different game to the safety of the cushioned lifestyle (sorry about the play on words) of snooker players; hence the prices on offer. There is no doubt whatsoever that there is more chance of a golf pro getting injured before a tournament than a snooker player but the layers have got away with murder down the years and punters are still queuing up to part with their money. This is part of the reason that the exchanges are proving so popular, particularly where golf is concerned.

Bookmakers will also defend their prices by suggesting that they are betting to around a 2% per runner scenario, which has long since been an accepted percentage by the industry. 2% a runner's terminology stems from the fact that, in any betting scenario, bookmakers are entitled to form a market which adds up to 2% over-round for each runner, player or participant. If ten runners go to post for a race at Brighton, for example, bookmakers are supposedly justified in betting to around 120%, which covers their 100% market in an ideal world, in addition to the 2% margin they apply for each runner.

Layers would suggest that an ideal world simply does not exist these days, as it is nigh impossible to get every runner in a race in the book, which has been determined by the increased knowledge of the punter from the internet and the media in general. Bookmakers quickly latch on to the point that in The Open Championship they are entitled to play to a 200+% market, with over 100 golfers contesting the tournament. To be entirely fair, the layers have got a point, because there is no rule 4 in operation in a sporting market, unlike the example race at Brighton. Moreover, the percentages for a ten runner race at Brighton these days will probably add up to no more than 115.9% on average.

If Tiger Woods is a 6/4 favourite for a tournament, there would be no rule 4 deduction from winning bets if a successful client has backed the winner at 10/1 before Tiger became a non-runner. Equally, punters would argue that their money is lost when a player fails to tee-off for any given reason, which all adds to the enemy stance adopted by punters against bookmakers the world over.

2006 witnesses the next Europe v USA competition for the Ryder Cup and the betting exchanges can expect plenty of business during the three-day tournament. More than any other sporting punter, the golf enthusiast has plenty of time on their hands to play the relevant markets on their computer because of the time the matches take to complete. I would argue that, played correctly, no punter should wind up losing on the final day of the Ryder Cup event, when there are twelve matches in play, with betting in running constantly available.

It might surprise readers to note that betting in running was not devised until 1995, yet so much of our staking is geared towards this part of the industry ten years later. As much as 95% of all cricket bets are taken in running according to one bookmaker, whilst other layers report that 50% of tennis revenue is created in play, with a quarter of football wagers staked within the 90 minutes of action.

What I like about golf and the Ryder Cup in particular is that, from a mental approach, the draw is not a variable in the eyes of the player. Bookmakers are compelled to price up the stalemate, which offers punters the edge as far as

I am concerned. In the single matches on the last day, for example, there is so much pressure on the first few players that go out to play, that form goes out of the window, as does the logic of layers on the exchanges at times. The advice is to get the best price about the player you fancy to win the match in question and look to back the draw (if you have to) on the exchanges, where a better price will undoubtedly become available, even if you have to wait for a few holes for the odds to develop.

You now have two parts of the equation covered and you simply have to sit and wait for the third scenario to develop one way or the other. Don't be frightened to develop negative equity on one or two matches throughout the day, just as long as you are in pin position in the rest of the matches.

The Art of Bookmaking is to put yourself ahead of the game as often as possible, even if it does not happen one hundred per cent of the time.

Cricket

2006 is also a big year in cricket terms as England head out to Australia towards the end of the year to defend the Ashes. We can only hope that the preparation for this tour is far better than the shambles that ensued for the Pakistan series, after England's cricketers had been dubbed as kings of sport by beating the old enemy on home soil back in the summer of 2005.

Yes, the England-Australia tests built into a pulsating series of matches but in hindsight, weren't Pakistan one of the best bets of all time to bring us back down to earth?

It is never easy to tour the sub-continent, let alone when

you have left your brains back in Trafalgar Square on top of an open topped bus and, to confound it all, the powers that be then suggested that the players could stay up half the night before a match to be treated like royalty at the BBC Sports Personality of the Year programme! Why couldn't the award have simply been pre-recorded? Captain Michael Vaughan was back in the studio because of an injury and could have talked the talk on behalf of the team, or perhaps I am missing the point here for a serious punt on Pakistan by all concerned!

The last point was made in jest by the way, as I fully accept it was just another shambles organised by the England cricket regime, which we tolerate for some reason.

Having been stung by the Ashes defeat, Australia will be up to all sorts of tricks to ensure that their current odds, 4/6 at the time of writing, are realistic. With England being offered at 2/1 and 9/2 available about the drawn series, I suggest that you beg, steal or borrow money to lump on Australia if you see the odds drift towards the even money mark. I would shorten the odds for the draw personally and my betting for the series would be 4/7 Australia – 3/1 The Draw – 7/2 England, bearing in mind that Vaughan's men will be going out to Australia with the psychological advantage that a drawn series is all they need to retain the trophy. Such thoughts will inevitably creep into their decision-making at some stage of the tour and if you can find quotes of 4/5 Australia and 11/2 the draw, you could invest the second mortgage money with collective (dutching) odds of 2/5.

Backing on county matches or championships is a different kettle of fish entirely, though value can be obtained if you treat the sport seriously.

Bookmakers were betting 3/1 Surrey – 7/2 Warwickshire – 5/1 Kent at the head of the market for the championship last season, before a ball had been bowled, which was perfectly fair to punters in the circumstances. Bearing in mind that there were another six teams for punters to potentially back in the division (at 7/1 upwards), the bookmakers were betting 8/13 for one of the three quoted teams to win the title.

Unlike tournament betting in other sports, layers have to protect their margins with just nine teams in the mix, especially when they are offering 1-2-3 place terms, albeit (understandably) at one fifth rules to finish in the frame.

You might find trouble lumping on any side that represents a bet to nothing, such as Kent in this instance, when prices of 5/1 or more are quoted. The bookmaker is potentially on a hiding to nothing, as just six other teams attempt to stop the gambled side finishing in the first three on behalf of the layer. Outside of pride and strong management, there simply isn't enough incentive for teams that find themselves out of the running after six to eight weeks of the championship, to battle hard to protect their fifth or sixth position in the league.

Similarly, bookmakers are alive to antics that might prevail when the individual odds for one-day matches are published in price comparisons in the Racing Post. Bookmakers are duty bound to lay the prices to fivers and tenners and are happy to accommodate punters when genuine followers of the sport are simply looking to add interest to the day's fayre.

These accountants know however, that whilst each individual company will get lucky on a 50-50 basis regarding which of the two over-round teams they lay, laying bets to accommodate burglars is the quick way to bankruptcy. The Art of Bookmaking is not about pricing up two-team matches, hoping that the punter you accommodated with one half of the equation has backed the winning team in the shop up the road.

Another factor that bookmakers might want to take into account in cricket bets, is to attempt to accommodate the two flies up the wall punters, who will quite literally bet on anything.

Imagine the scenario that England are playing Pakistan in a ODI (one day international) at Lords. As an example, usual odds might be offered as 8/11 England and evens Pakistan, according to the form of the two teams at the time. How could you as a bookmaker or layer offer more attractive odds on basically the same scenario of 9/4 − 5/2 − 5/2 − 10/3?

The added factor in this example shows how bookmakers or layers can utilise situations that are already in place with the toss of the coin. And yes, some punters are that sad, so don't become negative and ignore this opportunity as a bookmaker or layer.

If you remain positive you will comprehend that, by offering this bet within a bet, you can offer 4/6 England and 10/11 Pakistan (compared with the initial quotes of 8/11 and Evens), simply by offering more attractive odds! By deciding that both teams are equal in terms of winning the toss, the basic price for each scenario is 5/6, as in all match situations where a favourite cannot be determined.

To produce the new odds for the game, you simply multiply the 1.84 (5/6 − winning the toss) by the relevant price that you decide on the result of the toss. Logic suggests that the type of wicket favour the side that wins the toss but in this example we will simply deduce that the captain that calls correctly will see his team reduced in price, whereas the losing team will be at a slight disadvantage.

Four new prices emerge from a marketing perspective before the toss is made. Instead of offering the boring prices of 8/11 and Evens, you (the bookmaker) can offer:

9/4 England win the toss and the match
10/3 England win the toss but lose the match
5/2 Pakistan win the toss and the match
5/2 Pakistan win the toss but lose the match

The market you have created is fairly competitive at 11.1% over round, yet you have added interest to a bet that had lacked sparkle initially. Adding the two scenarios for England to win (9/4 & 5/2) equates to odds of 4/6, whilst Pakistan are on offer, from a dutching perspective, at 10/11.

Additional interest in the match alongside better margins to work with… and all for the toss of a coin! Offer the usual bets relating to the top batsmen and bowlers by all means but you might attract more interesting wagers using the 'toss' structure from heavier investors.

The Art of Bookmaking is to attract small and large investors alike, especially when the odds are in your favour. This is particularly the case in sports betting, when the percentages are on your side and there are no live animals ready to land a knockout blow.

Chapter 8

Cup Ties, Tournaments and Inventive Odds

The mathematics of bookmaking highlighted by the inventiveness of compiling odds when pricing up tournaments that are governed by round-by-round ties.

Tournament ante-post betting is a potentially volatile market, irrespective of whether you are pricing up football teams, snooker players or tennis rubbers. For the benefit of this example, I'm asking you to suppose you are pricing up the FA Cup market in different rounds and to realise exactly what you are asking potential punters to accept in terms of winning outright the individual ties as the competition progresses. As an example, a punter is basically accepting their chosen team as 4/6 chances to win every remaining round if their team are going to lift the trophy, if they take a price of 12/1 at the last 32 (fourth round) stage.

Many punters would describe 12/1 shots as being relative outsiders to win the trophy at the final 32 stage, yet the true odds of a team offered at such a price, is 4/6 for the team in question to win through their next five cup-ties. These outsiders are actual favourites to win through each of their six rounds if they are to win the cup. Don't believe me? Calculate 1.667 (the relevant price for 4/6) together five times and the result is 12.87... very nearly 12/1.

You will find these figures useful when betting or laying on a round-by-round basis:

Last 64 (third round of the F.A. Cup – six ties to win):

Price to win outright:	Actual odds to win each round:
13/2	2/5
8/1	4/9
10/1	1/2
12/1	8/15
16/1	8/13
20/1	4/6
25/1	8/11
33/1	4/5
40/1	5/6
50/1	10/11
66/1	Evens
100/1	6/5
200/1	11/8

Would you have supposed that the team you might have backed at 25/1 to win the cup competition, are actually 8/11 favourites to win on a round-by-round basis when the competition is opened up to the main teams? In fact the outright price needs to be 100/1 before the team are longer than Even money to win on a round-by-round basis.

Last 32 (fourth round – five ties to win):

5/1	4/9
6/1	1/2
8/1	4/7
12/1	4/6
16/1	4/5

20/1	5/6
33/1	21/20
40/1	11/10
50/1	6/5
100/1	6/4

Last 16 (fifth round – four ties to win):

10/3	4/9
4/1	1/2
5/1	4/7
6/1	8/13
7/1	4/6
8/1	8/11
10/1	4/5
12/1	10/11
16/1	21/20
20/1	11/10

Last 8 (quarter-finals – three ties to win):

9/4	1/2
11/4	4/7
10/3	8/13
4/1	8/11
9/2	4/5
6/1	10/11
8/1	11/10
10/1	5/4
14/1	6/4
16/1	13/8
20/1	7/4

How are prices made up at the semi-final stage of a tournament? Putting aside the running up money that might sway the odds, arithmetic takes over, pure and simple. Let's take four popular football teams as a guideline and work from there.

The imaginary neutral ground semi-finals of a tournament might be priced up from an outright perspective like this, on current form at the time of writing:

1/2 Chelsea v Liverpool 6/4
4/6 Man. Utd. v Arsenal 11/10

How do we arrive at the following odds to win the competition outright?

6/5 Chelsea
5/2 Man Utd
4/1 Arsenal
9/2 Liverpool

Taking each team in turn, we have to deduce what price the potential opposition would be if the sides in question made it through to the final. Listing the teams accordingly, these would be my prices prior to the semi-finals being played.

4/6 Chelsea to beat Manchester United
4/7 Chelsea to beat Arsenal

5/4 Liverpool to beat Manchester United
11/10 Liverpool to beat Arsenal

11/10 Manchester United to beat Chelsea
4/7 Manchester United to beat Liverpool

4/6 Arsenal to beat Liverpool

5/4 Arsenal to beat Chelsea.

Utilising the 1/2 odds of Chelsea beating Liverpool, we have to deduce the price of Chelsea meeting either Manchester United or Arsenal in the final. The obvious price in this instance is 8/13, which is the direct price in between 4/6 (against Manchester United) and 4/7 (against Arsenal). Multiply the two prices (1/2 and 8/13) together to give you resulting odds of 7/5.

The scenario for Manchester United is slightly more complicated, albeit the same basic principle applies. In this situation, we have split prices because, on the one hand United might be 11/10 chances against Chelsea but they would be favourites (4/7) to defeat Liverpool.

We always err on the side of the likelier result of the other semi-final given these situations, which suggests that we lean towards the even money mark for United as they will probably meet Chelsea in the final in this exercise.

Multiply the two prices for United together (4/6 – the price to beat Arsenal and the Even money odds we have deduced for the final), which equates to a price of more than 9/4 but less than 5/2. Given the fact that United will be second favourites in the final in all probability, I am happy to stretch the price out to 6/5. If, as is often the case with Manchester United, there is plenty of money in the book for them already, I would consider reducing the price to 9/4, easing out the favourites to 5/4 in those circumstances.

We use the same structure to determine the prices for Arsenal and Liverpool which completes the book.

Happy with those odds?

You shouldn't be! As in all betting scenarios, you must be prepared to carry out the spade work which should prove to you that the prices are correct. What is this spade work?

Evaluate the dutching principle to the odds you are offering which equate to the prices below. By offering 7/5 Chelsea – 5/2 Man Utd – 4/1 Arsenal – 9/2 Liverpool you are betting:

4/11 Chelsea or Man Utd will win the trophy
8/15 Chelsea or Arsenal
4/7 Chelsea or Liverpool
21/20 Manchester United or Arsenal
11/10 Manchester United or Liverpool
13/8 Arsenal or Liverpool

1/16 Chelsea – Man Utd – Arsenal will lift the cup
1/12 Chelsea – Man Utd – Liverpool
1/5 Chelsea – Arsenal – Liverpool
1/2 Man Utd – Arsenal – Liverpool

If you are happy offering those prices, then and only then, should you release the prices to the press. And you thought that compiling prices was a breeze eh? The best prices for the FA Cup this year (2006) before the third round stage were as follows:

Chelsea: 7/2 (2/7)
Manchester United: 9/2 (1/3)
Arsenal: 6/1 (between 2/5 & 4/11)
Liverpool: 9/1 (between 1/ 2 & 4/9)
Tottenham: 14/1 (4/7)
Newcastle: 25/1 (8/11)
Middlesbrough: 28/1 (between 4/5 & 8/11)
Manchester City: 33/1 (4/5)

Everton: 40/1 (5/6)
Aston Villa: 40/1 (5/6)
Bolton: 50/1 (10/11)
Blackburn: 50/1 (10/11)
Birmingham: 66/1 (Evens)
Charlton: 66/1 (Evens)
Fulham: 66/1 (Evens)

The prices in brackets were the odds for each team to win through the six ties required to lift the trophy. There were a few Premiership casualties at the first hurdle, none more so than Tottenham who were regarded as 4/7 chances to win through each of their six games if Jol's men were to go on and lift the trophy.

The fact that Tottenham were 1/7 chances to win the game after 40 minutes at the Walker Stadium when 2-0 up against Leicester, is a great example of how ante-post betting on the FA Cup (and many other tournament situations) is fraught with danger. Ask anybody who took a price for Glasgow Celtic to win the Scottish Cup this season!

It will be an interesting exercise to examine how the prices worked out by the time you are reading this book. The last 16 teams in the Champions League were known at the time of writing and my mind goes back twelve months to a suggestion I made to the Tote.

I didn't realise at the time that the nanny did not own the rights to create a pool relating to football matches but the day will come very soon when punters will have another choice to make regarding their punting on soccer. I suggest that the last 16 phase in the Champions League is the perfect time to create a massive pool, as far as outright winners in each individual match is concerned.

The following wager is particularly attractive in my opinion, as the potential client can afford to be wrong with two selections, yet pick up a dividend anyway.

Consider wagering a pre-determined stake (perhaps ten pounds a unit) on deciding which of the following teams will win through to the last eight.

Benfica v Liverpool
PSV v Bayern Munich
AC Milan v Lyon
Real Madrid v Arsenal
Ajax v Inter Milan
Chelsea v Barcelona
Rangers v Villarreal
Werder Bremen v Juventus

It's easy in hindsight to look at the tournament now you know the results but would this bet have appealed to you before the last 16 matches had been played? The pool bet would reward customers who had successfully predicted at least six of the eight ties correctly. Monies (at ten pounds per unit) would be pooled together and the dividends could be paid out (after deductions) at the following rates:

60% of the pool could be split between the punters who had forecast all eight matches correctly.
30% of the pool could be divided between clients who called seven teams correctly.
10% of the pool could be split between punters who chose 6/8 teams who were successful from an aggregate score perspective.

Perhaps a rollover scenario could exist if all punters had

failed to call all eight matches correctly. After all, the full 2 x 2 x 2 x 2 x 2 x 2 x 2 x 2 equates to a 255/1 accumulator and as a famous player (Jimmy Greaves) once said, 'it's a funny old game!'

Alternatively, the company who accommodated the wager might decide that the pool should be split, with 75% of the money going to clients who had predicted seven correct results, with the other 25% being shared by those with six correct nominations. The joy of a pool bet such as this is that, providing you have called at least six of the matches correctly, your reward is unknown.

The national lottery (for all its flaws) has proved that punters don't mind the uncertainty of the potential reward, just as long as they are in the queue when winnings are paid out.

The scenario is a winner given that the final eight matches are played in two legs over two nights; ensuring maximum interest is maintained. Investors with access to Sky TV can follow nearly all the matches live on television to increase their enjoyment. Bookmakers and layers could also be on to a winner, by attracting business on the final night of the games in question, with people wanting to hedge their bets when a punter deems themself to be in a decent position at the half way stage. The pool operator might also consider opening up a pool for the final night's (second leg) business, attracting wagers where the final four places in the quarter-finals are determined.

Going back to the original idea, I think we should consider that as at least six correct forecasts are required (63/1 at even money odds per tie), the potential reward would be high enough to attract and more importantly re-attract second leg, potential investors.

CHAPTER 9

Tennis and Side Issues

Tennis only comes alive from a betting perspective when the cameras visit SW19 and even then only from a laying viewpoint.

This has been the case for a few years now since the advent of the betting exchanges, as astute punters have made hay whilst the showers continued to rain down on Tim Henman. Who in their right mind could have ever backed this underachiever, for all his undoubted talent?

I guess the tennis faithful will be hoping that Tim and Andrew Murray lock horns at Wimbledon this year and at the time of writing, I couldn't separate the pair from an odds compiler's viewpoint. Andy beat Tim towards the back end of 2005 but surely Tim's experience of the grass courts would counteract that scenario. If the pair met up, I would attempt to create some extra revenue by offering these odds, if I was still unable to split the pair at the time.

Tim Henman to win the first set and the match: 6/4
Andrew Murray to win the first set and the match: 6/4
Henman to win the first set and lose the match: 5/1
Murray to win the first set and lose the match: 5/1

In adding the percentages together, we are suggesting that the player who wins the first set is 1/4 to go on and win the match. Conversely, the said player is 2/1 to lose the game.

These prices are a little tight (113.4%) but it is difficult to argue against the odds on offer. The prices were compiled from the base fact that the two players were 5/6 to win the game.

I then decided that the player that had won the first set had been elevated from a 54% chance of winning the tie, to around the 75% mark, or a 1/3 shot in terms of odds. Multiplying the original odds of 5/6 by the new 1/3 status offers us the quoted price of 6/4, whilst the negative quote of 5/1 is evaluated by the contrasting odds of 5/6 and 9/4 (losing the first set).

If you wanted to become competitive, you might go 13/8 on either nominated player winning the first set and going on to win the match, which equates to a far more acceptable 109.6% from the potential punter's viewpoint.

How do bookmaker's price up set betting between two players? Let's take a scenario where two players are priced up at 1/2 and 6/4. We will call the players Borg and Connors to add some spice to proceedings!

The two percentages equate to a book of 106.7%. By using the same formula as we utilised in the snooker frame betting example either way, we need that basic figure 106.7% to work from. Given the tennis Grand Slam scenario that there are six prices to offer, 3-0 – 3-1 – 3-2, let's adopt a stance where we are looking to bet to 114.9%.

We need to find the figure with which to multiply the basic odds (1/2 and 6/4) and the way to go about this is exactly the same way that we did in the snooker example. By dividing the required percentage figure of 114.9% by the original 106.7%, we deduce that the multiplication figure in this instance is 1.0768.

We now multiply the base percentages 66.7% (Borg) and 40.0% (Connors) by the 1.0768 result, which now means that we can bet to 71.8% (Borg) and 43.1% (Connors).

In exactly the same way as we compiled the frame prices for the snooker example, the prices could now be offered along these lines:

BORG	SETS	CONNORS
3/1	3-0	14/1
9/4	3-1	6/1
11/2	3-2	7/2
=71.8%		=43.1%

I priced this match up by suggesting that the game was unlikely to reach the fifth set (percentages added together equate to a 12/5 chance of that scenario occurring). I am further suggesting that a whitewash (85/40) is unlikely, whereby the percentages are geared towards either player winning by a margin of 3-1 (10/11).

We can only rely on our memories in this example of course but I'm quite happy to suggest that Connors would always have found it difficult to whitewash Borg, though the reverse situation is nowhere near as unlikely.

Equally, you will note that, if the match was destined to reach a fifth set, the odds differential between the two players is markedly reduced. The fact that Connors is classed as a 7/2 chance to win after a fifth set had been contested, does not mean that he would be favourite to win the decider if the first four sets had been evenly shared. The 11/2 quote for

Borg simply advertises my belief that Borg would win either 3-0 or 3-1, which equates to a price of 4/5.

By reducing the 11/2 quote for Borg to win 3-2, you would be offering an even money scenario (or bigger) about the Swede winning either 3-0 or 3-1, which would plainly be wrong, especially given his original 1/2 quote to win the match.

It's important to have a genuine interest in the scenario where you are offering odds, so keep situations like a general election on a back burner if you have no particular penchant for politics.

Advertise average prices by all means but don't get too involved in laying prices that the sharks are trying to obtain. These people might specialise on a given subject, whereas you are merely offering prices without having the correct knowledge to back up such odds.

By average prices I refer to the middle ground you should be offering. If the Labour party are being offered between 2/5 and 1/3 for example, offer 4/11 which will keep any critics quiet. By not offering the shortest price in the village, you can refer cynics to the company offering 1/3, whilst you will keep the sharks away by taking the sensible route. The advice is simply not to get involved in major punts where you have little or no knowledge.

If you are seeking to accommodate lumpy bets such as this, you must be doing something wrong with the bread and butter side of the business. All you should need to convince you that this is good advice, is to realise how much hard work might be shed to produce a productive Bank Holiday Monday, only for a shrewdie to come in late doors and rob you of your hard earned wedge in one fell swoop.

'Moderation in all things' doesn't only refer to alcohol and 'George Best' lifestyles. Moderation in bookmaking is hard to come by these days, as any layer at a greyhound stadium will testify. The best days invariably occur at greyhound stadiums when the bookmaker is accommodating a large crowd at a bank holiday meeting, when families come along with their fivers and tenners trying to get lucky. As a bookmaker, all you are relying on is the percentages to work as they should and invariably you will come away from the track with a decent profit.

Unfortunately these meetings are few and far between nowadays and layers are lucky to lay three dogs in a race, let alone all six. The families are up in the restaurant staking their small wagers on the tote, whilst the sharks move in on the books, with invariably just two greyhounds on their minds between them. Yes, you might have the odd brilliant night when you get the majority of bets beaten but more often than not, your books become unbalanced.

In this scenario, you are not acting as a bookmaker as such, more a punter hoping selective dogs are beaten, rather than gaining your margin from the percentages that should be working on your behalf. Similarly in shops, bookmakers will invariably survive if they have a unit that attracts the mug money (though there is far less of that around now) such as lucky fifteen bets and the like.

I used to manage shops for a small chain in West London many years ago and the best outlet in percentage terms was the unit that consistently attracted relatively small money from thousands of slips.

The first outlet that was sold off by the company was the one that produced a far higher turnover from less than a third of the number of slips of the best shop.

'Moderation in all things' in bookmaking terms means a balanced book.

CHAPTER 10

Betting Exchanges

One of the few people in the horse racing world that, in my opinion, had his finger on every pulse was former Midlands away bookmaker Don Butler. I cannot recall exactly how it happened but Don contacted me in the late eighties, shortly after I wrapped up a small business called 'Nationwide Naps'.

I won't go into every detail of the idea, though it was based on the naps table that used to appear in the Sporting Life on a daily basis.

I came up with the idea of forming a competition based on punters ringing in their nap selection on a daily basis, where investors could win pool prizes based on regions of the country and the nation as a whole. It was relatively successful early doors but people soon tired of the request to telephone their entry every day and the rest is history.

John Francome kindly presented one of the national prizes over a luncheon event in Swindon one Sunday and whether it was John that passed on the idea to Channel 4 eventually I'm not sure, suffice to say that a similar competition – Channel 4 Champion Tipster Competition – runs to this day on a premium line payment, which started up shortly after the demise of my company. Either way, John gave his time for nothing and we all enjoyed a wonderful afternoon, whilst what has resulted since for Channel 4 has left me comfortable with the thought that I can dream up good ideas on a regular basis.

Don Butler somehow got hold of my number and we arranged to meet at Hereford one day when he was standing as the away bookmaker. Despite the fact that Nationwide Naps had gone to the wall, he liked the idea and thought the two of us should put our heads together for potential future use. Don might have got carried away with the idea that I was a money-man, which couldn't have been further from the truth and, whilst we had some interesting discussions over the following months, nothing really came of our association. It was when watching Don work at Hereford however, that I realised that laying off money could be turned into a positive scenario rather than a negative one.

Don transported good friends to the races who he utilised as his laying off bookmakers. The friendships remained intact despite the fact that money was involved, for one major reason. No bookmaker ever laid off money on horses wanting the relevant beast to score. The friends would be unanimous in wanting the horse in question to get beaten, hence Don was happy to pay his friends at the end of the day when the ledgers were audited.

Why give the money to faceless people at the end of a telephone, when he could line the pockets of mates? This was the inevitable outcome of course, because so many independent bookmakers would still be in business today but for laying off money on horses which were destined to lose.

The Catch 22 scenario has been in place for independent

bookmakers since 1961 and, whilst the small layer remains in business, the situation is a realistic part of daily transactions.

Away bookmakers disappeared from the racecourses as a result of the 1998 decision of the National Joint Pitch Committee who finally put the nail in the coffin of the away layers, usually residing towards the back row of the assembled bookmaking joints.

Until 1998, punters had the opportunity of betting in the on-course betting shops as they do today but competition was rife from Don and one or two others who were fighting for their share of the business or the away meetings. Don rightly held the belief that he wanted favourites or popular horses to win at the track where he was standing, so that punters could play up their winnings in his joint a few minutes later.

That first day at Hereford was a learning curve for yours truly, not only in horse racing terms but also because we made our way to Hall Green Greyhound Stadium directly after the last race at breakneck speed. Don had stood as a bookmaker at Hall Green for many years and he eventually passed on the lucky hod to me when I began trading at Ramsgate many years later. The hod was not so lucky for yours truly!

We popped into his lovely Redditch home in between the two venues for a quick bite to eat, relating the afternoon's business to Don's wife. One of Don's golden rules to this day is to be honest with the other half, always trying to keep her happy, both with the truth and some money to buy some shoes from time to time.

A few years after our initial meeting, Don and I met up at the Metropole Hotel at Birmingham's Exhibition

Centre near the International Airport, to discuss his idea for a new newspaper to compete with the Racing Post. Don had nothing against the Racing Post but thought that competition was vital for the industry to grow as a whole. As I intimated in my opening sentence in this chapter, Don was invariably ahead of his time. I had only known two people in the newspaper industry unfortunately and didn't have much to offer towards the conversation.

Jim Sollis was one of the leading marketing men at the old Sporting Life newspaper when I was getting Nationwide Naps off the ground, whilst Neil Cook was the editor of the sister publication The Sporting Life Weekender. These two men helped to launch Nationwide Naps onto an unsuspecting public and, such was their help and expertise, that they were in no way responsible for the eventual demise of the company. It's funny how life works out, because I finally tracked Jim down last summer (2005) when we met for supper one evening, whilst Neil Cook is being drafted in to work on The Sportsman project.

Neil had been head-hunted to work in North America as far as I knew and yet again I am amazed at the merry-go-round of the racing business. Don hasn't any involvement with The Sportsman to my knowledge (though you never know with him), as he now plays the betting exchanges on a daily and professional basis.

I shouldn't think there is a more professional player of the exchanges than Don and the plus side for his wife, is that she can keep tabs on her husband now! Don readily admits to being a lucky man, even if things have gone pear-shaped now and then.

He was in at the start of the game when betting shops opened and, more by luck than judgment, Don was set to change direction at just the right time to accommodate the exchanges when they became popular. You can't be lucky all the time however and Don has survived by taking chances, though they would always have been calculated risks, which is a different thing entirely from Joe Soap who is chancing his arm in a business he has not studied.

I look forward to the day when Don has his autobiography published, though it would be the longest read you have ever encountered. Lord of the (silver) Rings? Not quite perhaps but the publication would be a bloody good read.

I get a great buzz from thinking that my books might be purchased whilst I am tucked up safely in bed and the same situation applies to offering odds on the exchanges.

You can personally trade without having to be awake, which is about as good as it gets in my book!

This is one of the positive sides to the new technology, though for every plus factor, just as many negative comments will be fired at people who appreciate additional betting opportunities to those offered by traditional bookmakers. Ignore the nonsense you have heard from some of the bookmakers who suggest that betting exchanges are a threat to the industry as a whole. Yes, I worry that the sport as a whole might suffer because horses can now be backed to lose.

There is an element of risk regarding every aspect of the horse racing business and, as betting exchanges are not going to disappear, we might as well accept them as part of everyday punting and stop running scared of new technology. What the bookmakers have been saying is that the integrity of the sport is open to question, though they conveniently forget to mention that the exchanges are another way of marking their card before races are run.

A friend recently exclaimed that bookmakers were being fair by offering prices for every race after a certain hour in the morning, which couldn't be further from the truth. Many layers have gone to the wall down the years by laying early prices but bookmakers now have the protection of the terminals that have already given them a strong indication to every race on the day. Contrary to what my friend suggested, bookmakers have actually saved money through the information technology now available. Because of their considerable skill, the tissue men were well paid in their day but in reality, who needs such employees nowadays?

Few of us go to war (from either side of the trenches) without the aid of advice from one source or another but if a layer has been told that a certain horse can be backed or laid by his whisperer, the first thing the bookmaker will do is go and check it out on his laptop.

As I'm writing these few paragraphs on Christmas Eve, I've been reliably informed by the media weather boys and girls that frost followed by snow is in the offing and that Sandown is to hold an inspection on Boxing Day morning for the King George meeting.

Such words would normally find me reaching for the sauce but I've logged on to the Betfair site to discover that racing going ahead is being backed at 1.09, whilst the abandoned scenario is available at 7.2.

I'm far happier to see what layers and backers are doing with their leftover Christmas money, than to tune in to Dolly Daydream, who for some reason is anxious to tell you her name before she reads out her latest information to an expectant public! The lady is the winner either way however, as 'Dolly' is a nigh certainty to appear on Big Sister before too long... who is going to offer me 14's?

You catch my point, of course, which is that unless you live in the immediate area of Esher, who would have invested much money a few years ago given the uncertainty of conditions in the region?

I can sleep peacefully knowing that some big punter has an Uncle Harry living in the Surbiton area who has been on the wire with accurate information. For all that information and informed opinion goes astray from time to time, would you rather listen to Tanya's IT information on Channel Four, or watch John McCririck pointing to his nose suggesting that the layers are going bottle about the favourite.

Who needs such outdated nonsense?

I've been in touch with many of the presenters, producers and directors of televised racing coverage, offering to extend information that you have found in this book to the general public but to a person (phrasing being politically correct) the programme planners have kicked potential information to punters into touch.

Can somebody out there convince me that a punter would prefer watching John McCririck's antics of relating up the arm and ear hole remarks, rather than learn the effect of what percentages could do for their pocket given such knowledge?

I remember hearing about a tournament poker player who had won in excess of ten thousand pounds at the table and his immediate move after securing his swag was to invest in several hundred pounds worth of books in order to gain more knowledge. I like and admire his attitude. By perusing the exchanges on a daily basis, we can learn more about the business from a relatively new perspective and you can bet that the bookmakers who survive modern technology will be the layers who used it to their advantage from day one. Bookmakers also make use of informed clients who mark their cards on a daily basis. The big companies are happy to accommodate punters who make a profit out of betting, providing the information is useful to them on a larger scale.

The layers will not stand Joe Soap and his mates continually making a living from the game but, if a professional is involved, they are willing to let the punter become a loss leader for a while.

The major company that I worked for as an odds compiler accommodated a leading international footballer who was privy to top class information from one of the biggest stables in the land.

The player concerned used to ring up with large wagers, which simply marked the cards for the company.

The punter eventually went into the red and disappeared to my knowledge, suggesting that, for all the information a client can glean, the odds are still stacked in the bookmaker's favour.

I think the phrasing of that last sentence is the key to potential bookmakers and layers making a living from playing the betting exchanges. Stick to the odds being in your favour, rather than trying to stand out from the crowd by attracting money that others are not willing to lay. Personally, I'm not interested in playing or laying bets that are structured around a horse that might or might not recover from a last fence blunder, that will lead to victory or defeat on the run-in.

The problem with laying in running is that you need a very sharp mind, which does not apply to the author of this book.

Like many people, I am fine when given the time to construct a detailed plan of attack but I wouldn't like to be rushed into making decisions on the racing front on the exchanges. Laying a price about a golfer with ten holes to play is one thing, offering a price about a horse with two furlongs to run in a sprint event is something entirely different. Stories of layers offering daft prices about horses are commonplace now and the Kicking King saga relating to last year's Cheltenham Gold Cup should be the warning for all of us to heed.

In an earlier chapter, you will remember that I pointed out that 'one see is worth a thousand hears' (dreadful translation of the words from Confucius I know) and never were these words more valid that when Tom Taafe stated that the Blue Riband winner would not run at Prestbury Park. Smart Alec's jumped onto the situation, offering odds of 999-1 compared to the previous day's offer of 7/2 and the rest is history. If you want to make a quick few bucks here and there and speculate with rumour or gossip, the betting exchange is not the place to trade.

If you want to lay all one hundred and sixty three golfers at a two-bit tournament however, craic on! I know a few people that literally work a four-day week laying and playing the exchanges on golf tournaments from both sides of the Atlantic Ocean.

If I had to offer one piece of advice to readers who had plenty of money to invest on the exchanges, it would be to set up your own bank, manage it professionally and concentrate on golf. Don't ask me where to go from there, because I simply don't know enough about the sport to gamble your finances away but what I do know, is that there is enough information, from Keith Elliott and others, who can steer you in the right direction.

The other piece of advice if you take this option, is not to be greedy and simply take your potential profit from the odds which, I repeat, are in your favour as a layer. For all that I would love to offer exchange advice on horse racing and football (my two great loves in sport), there are logical reasons to avoid investing great sums of money in both instances. Whilst I lean heavily on the stats that I have talked about in this publication and for all my forty years of involvement, I have yet to speak to a horse. That statement should need no clarification.

If you require further proof, seek out the punters that had played the ante-post Cheltenham Festival markets with Trabolgan, Kicking King, Inglis Drever, Rathgar Beau, Well Chief, possibly Harchibald and other horses that will not make it to the start of the relevant events at Prestbury Park in March 2006.

I can hear the layers of these horses screaming that it was easy money to earn but the people who laid the likes of Kingscliff, Beef Or Salmon and Monkerhostin at inflated prices might be screaming for other reasons! You will appreciate once again, that these points were valid at the time of writing and might not necessarily be the case now.

Football is another sport that creates a huge amount of business on the exchanges but how can you invest in total confidence when just one player (of eleven) can make a monumental mistake to change the course of a game. Compare the two scenarios to that of golf and you will hopefully see my point.

Outside of the caddie and coach (and the Ryder Cup of course), golf is not a team game where outside influences can dramatically turn an event. Golf does not involve horses and greyhounds, animals that might just fancy an off day but are unable to tell backers or layers of their potential plight, whilst both horse racing and football do not have 100 odd runners on the bookmaker's (layer's) side, there are plenty of advantages to be gained through a professional approach to golf.

Horses for courses is a major factor, along with current form of the relevant players you would like to lay or back. There is not only the opportunity to lay prices back at any stage but more importantly, four days in which to do so. I'm not aware of many players that lead tournaments from start to finish and the ability to balance your books in running is prevalent in golf to such a degree that it cannot be compared to any other sport.

The time to speculate on horse racing (if you have to) is as a player rather than a layer. If you fancy a horse from an ante-post perspective after it has run well but not too well if you catch my drift, in a prep race, speculate on taking a large price about the beast in question and, if it is not in the list of runners, gamble on the horse taking its chance by asking for a layer to accommodate a couple of quid in three figure terms.

Gamble, if you must, on other people being greedy, not the other way around.

CHAPTER 11

Survival

A recent survey suggested that over 60% of punters were not worried about actually winning money, being more interested in the thrill of the chase. This merely demonstrates my belief that punters would latch on to some of the ideas I have put forward in this publication.

There are some even more bizarre ideas forthcoming, so hang on to your hats! The first scenario involves horse racing and the second is a direct challenge to bookmakers to take on the exchanges by offering inventive wagers along the same lines that are available online.

Imagine that eight runners are lining up for a novice chase over three miles at Sandown and the bookmakers are offering the following odds:

6/4 – 11/4 – 6/1 – 15/2 – 10/1 – 16/1 – 20/1 – 33/1.

How could bookmakers offer the same horses at the following odds?

7/2 – 11/2 – 11/1 – 14/1 – 18/1 – 28/1 – 33/1 – 50/1.

The bookmakers could offer these lucrative odds betting

with a bet within the original wager.

The structure of the extended odds is based upon all eight horses surviving the first circuit of the race. All eight runners must still be contesting the event as the field passes the winning post on the same circuit.

How are such odds evaluated?

It's down to odds compiling yet again, as the layer evaluates what chance all eight novices have of safely negotiating the first eleven fences before passing the winning post first time around. The odds for a field of novice chasers surviving those first eleven fences would differ from that of a line up of seasoned steeplechasers, whilst the number of runners also comes into play.

A bookmaker must always take in every scenario in order to survive; hence they must ensure that no fences were due to be dolled off before flag-fall. Using Sandown as an example again, it's worth noting that the pond fence (third last on the final circuit) and the open ditch in front of the stands are occasionally omitted.

The pond fence is a problem at certain times of the year, because the setting sun tends to shine right at the obstacle late in the afternoon. Similarly, the open ditch which is jumped with just a furlong or so to go on the first circuit in steeplechase events, is subject to poor ground conditions and in the event of a heavy frost or prolonged rain, the fence can be dolled off.

If bookmakers believe the price to be 4/5 (a 56% chance – rounded up) against all eight runners negotiating every obstacle safely, he simply multiplies those 4/5 odds with the original prices about the eight runners, though this is where the situation becomes interesting.

Given that we simply multiply the prices up as suggested

the odds become extended.

6/4 – 7/2 (6/4 x 4/5 = 7/2)
11/4 – 11/2
6/1 – 11/1
15/2 – 14/1
10/1 – 18/1
16/1 – 28/1
20/1 – 33/1
33/1 – 50/1

What other scenario comes into play?

The interesting part of the evaluation concerns the fact that, given all eight runners will have negotiated the first eleven fences safely, what would be the prices of the eight runners at the time, irrespective of how well they might be travelling in the race? Ignoring the 4/5 scenario for a moment, how would bookmakers be betting before the race, in the knowledge that all eight runners were going out onto the second circuit?

This is where mind games start to come into the equation, because shouldn't the favourite now drift given this situation, bearing in mind that all seven of their opponents are still standing and equally, could the prices of the outsiders recede considerably given the scenario?

This makes the potential wager all the more interesting, because different layers might have contrasting thoughts having digested such details. What is the advantage to the layer by offering the extended prices?

This is where greed (the bookmakers lethal weapon) comes into play, as the more observant amongst you will already have realised that the layers would scoop the entire book if just one horse failed to survive the first circuit. The lure for the punter revolves around the fact that better odds are available, which might seem particularly attractive if a punter has failed to back a winner before the race in question.

I guess a bookmaker could simply price up singular odds of 4/5 the field remaining intact over the first eleven fences but that doesn't set the pulse racing by comparison to going 7/2 the field in an eight horse event.

The football example could be utilised for the 2006 World Cup Finals and relates to handicapping on a time of goal(s) basis. Using England against Paraguay as an example, Paraguay might be offered a 17 minute handicap. Using the goal times printed in the trade press the next day, bookmakers would pay out on the team which amasses the most minutes from the goals that are scored in the match.

If England officially won the game by scoring in the 18th and 32nd minutes during the match, they would be deemed as losing this betting match if they conceded a goal in the 46th minute. England would score 50 points by adding the 18 and 32 minutes together, totalling a score of 50 minutes. Paraguay would score 63 with their 46th minute goal and their handicap advantage of 17.

The handicap would be dictated by the bookmakers who would attempt to bring the two teams together, using the chosen number of advantage in terms of minutes. The team receiving the handicap could be deemed as the winning nation if the game finished 0-0 at the end of ninety minutes play, dependent on the bookmaker's rules.

Odds could be offered accordingly:

10/11 England – 5/6 Paraguay – 66/1 The Draw.

Another bookmaker might like to attract punters to back (or oppose) England by offering Paraguay 12 minutes and 20 minutes respectively where they might chalk up prices as follows:

8/11 England – 11/10 Paraguay (+ 12 mins) – 50/1 The Draw

21/20 England – 5/6 Paraguay (+ 20 mins) – 50/1 The Draw.

The attraction to the punter remains constant throughout the 90 minutes whichever odds are offered, because the bet is never won (or lost) until the referee signals the end of play.

John McCririck doesn't help the industry when talking utter garbage, which he does from time to time. You will probably accuse me of doing much the same regarding parts of this book but I'm not the one up on the winner's rostrum suggesting that I know it all and representing the entire sport when it comes to betting. John spouted off about the people at Coral knowing that a horse was going to win at Sandown in one of the early televised races of 2006. It's a phrase that he often spouts after a race when he's calling the starting prices of the placed horses after an event.

'Corals knew,' he spouted about the 7/1 winner, as Tony McCoy dismounted the horse in the unsaddling enclosure.

Coral didn't know John, they simply compiled their prices and happened to be the shortest price in the village... that's all. If the compiler(s) knew, would they still be working with the Barking based outfit? Truth is, that a Racing Post employee telephones the compilers of all the leading bookmakers, asking for their quotes on the various early price races for the following day. Yes, somebody will invariably quote the shortest price on behalf of their company but it's pure theatre to suggest that the person responsible knew what was going to win the race and John should represent the sport to better effect.

I worked with the Channel 4 team throughout the Cheltenham Festival meeting a few years back, when I was asked by Andrew Franklin to create facts and figures relating to the three days of racing, which popped up on the screen from time to time. The entire team was invited into a room after the Morning Line programme on the first day (Tuesday), to ensure that everybody knew their respective duties for the three-day event.

Something had held Andrew up that morning and a few minutes ticked beyond ten o'clock when Big Mac ranted that he had other things to do and did not appreciate sitting on his (considerable) backside waiting for the meeting to start. Everyone to a person had plenty to do that morning as you might imagine, with three of the biggest days of racing on the calendar set before them but John was the only person to create a fuss. John has earned his right to be at the top of the tree in the betting jungle but my word, he can be a pain in the backside at times. Like so many other people in this sport, John generalises too much, especially on his comments about bookmaking.

If a short priced favourite has been beaten, John is the first to suggest that the bookmakers have had it off, totally misinterpreting the fact that bookmakers all have different ledgers to offer following a race. Yes, it's a rule of thumb that the layers will have a better day when the majority of favourites have been beaten but try telling that to an independent bookmaker who has laid a £1,000 to 50 bet about a 20/1 winner on the second or third row of the books on a wet and windy Monday afternoon at Plumpton!

The industry as a whole is wrong to suppose that all bookmakers look forward to their busiest day of the year, presuming that the Grand National holds pride of place in the calendar. Yes, I have managed several shops that record the Aintree fixture as the busiest day of the year though, equally, I have reported negative figures after the day's business to head office on many occasions.

I mentioned Johnny White (of the West London company Hooper & Cox) in an earlier chapter and time upon time John would dread another major fixture looming on the calendar, holding the belief that bookmaking (moreover profits) was all about laying bread and butter wagers to loyal punters at run of the mill meetings.

Conversely, I know of shops in the City of London that might as well remain closed for business on the first Saturday in April, such is the lack of interest in the area.

I was visiting a Coral's shop off Chancery Lane in London on the last day of the Royal Ascot meeting in 2005 and was amazed to learn that the unit might take as few as 50 bets on the day. Conversely, I know of a William Hill shop in the Cumbernauld region of Glasgow that allegedly used to take 1000 football coupons a week in their shop, such was the interest in soccer in that part of the world.

It's a case of horses for courses yet again and another reason why we should not generalise about this wonderful sport of kings. Betting shop managers and bookmakers are guilty of not helping themselves on a big day like the Grand

National. It took me years to realise that I could make my life a lot easier on Grand National day by bending the rules a little.

One year, I asked my girlfriend to write the name of one Grand National runner on a slip 50 or 60 times and repeated the request for every runner in the race. The slips were on display throughout the shop Grand National morning, whereby punters were directed towards their particular fancy, simply having to add their stake to complete the wager.

Betting shop staff are not allowed to write out bets as you might understand, hence the reason for asking my girlfriend to work the oracle on my behalf. The reason for the outrageous demand, was that I could simply have up to 40 piles of listed horses in front of me during the race, which I would discard as the runners fell by the wayside during the race. By the time the horses had crossed the finishing line, all I had to do was settle the four piles of lists, with literally hundreds of betting slips ignored in the process. With other shops asking punters to wait for anything up to an hour to be paid out after the result, I had finished settling literally within a few minutes!

We keep hearing that budgets are the be all and end all of business these days, yet I can envisage area managers throughout the country screaming at my beating the system by employing my girlfriend on behalf of the company at the time. The bookmakers would be up in arms about a manager organising a Grand National day in such a fashion but how can it be wrong when settling mistakes can be brought to a standstill by using a little ingenuity?

Equally, why can't bookmakers break the law to a fashion by having a little forethought before big races like the Grand National and the Cheltenham Gold Cup? I made the point about busy or quiet shops for different reasons a few paragraphs ago and bookmakers in the main are guilty of waiting for the public to come to them.

This is where generalising is wrong again, because a shop in a city centre might be potentially busy for the Gold Cup on a Friday (when the race now takes place) but substantially quieter for the Grand National on a Saturday. Bookmakers have just waited for the figures to roll in year on year, failing to address the individual requirements of different shops within their chain of outlets.

The law has restricted businesses from advertising down the years but if I had a shop in the centre of a busy 'office town' nowadays, I would consult local printers and arrange a special coupon to become available and then distribute the betting opportunities to all businesses in the local area. I would make the coupon easy to understand where boxes simply had to be ticked alongside the name of the relevant horse(s), which simply required the unit stake to be added.

We live in a competitive world, so why wait for customers to come to the bookmakers? Hooper & Cox were successful with their inventive trade from London Airport, some ten miles down the road from their Brentford base. A runner used to visit the airport every day at one o'clock (earlier in the winter months) and return with hoards of bets from the various workers assembled at Heathrow. Dickie drove back the next day with the relevant returns and the exercise was worth another shop in terms of profit margin. Outside of petrol costs and the wear and tear of the vehicle, there were no bills to pay, no staff to hire and practically every pound that was gained remained in the non existent cash register.

I remember back to the days when companies only laid the first goal scorer bets on televised matches. Along with another colleague, I started to compile prices for all the first division games as they were then, knowing the bet to be a real winner from the bookmaker's perspective. I used to offer my dubious skills to an independent bookmaker in West London and still wake up in a cold sweat when I recall another of my fanciful ideas.

Dave Collet used to have the shop opposite Sky Studios in Isleworth, which traded under the name of Middlesex Turf. It was one of Dave's shops that Lindsay and I bought in the area, which we turned into Great West Racing, referred to earlier in this publication. I was in the Middlesex Turf shop one late afternoon and Liverpool were due to play Nottingham Forest in a league game that evening. Going behind the counter and grabbing a piece of chalk (yes it was a long time ago), I started to write up a price about every individual player to score that evening. It was revolutionary stuff you understand, before the first goal scorer betting had even come into play on non-televised games.

The legendary Tom Finney had been in the crowd at Anfield that night and was asked his thoughts about Liverpool's 9-0 demolition of Forest after the game. The comments were slightly different to those made by Dave about my pricing up individual players for the first time on the night that Liverpool scored nine goals!

Dave survived though, basically because he wasn't scared of losing a few quid from novelty wagers. Can you imagine the number of bets he took on individual players on the next match? How have you coped with the arithmetic so far? Here's a final equation for you to determine.

Consider these Premiership matches and work out what bet is on offer by the odds that follow:

Manchester United v Tottenham
Liverpool v Everton
Arsenal v Bolton
Manchester City v Chelsea

33/1 None
5/1 One
13/8 Two
13/8 Three
11/2 All four

Have you determined the wager yet?

The bet asked of you is to name how many of the favourites will win? I have offered example prices to work on and by now you should know that the only way to accurately equate odds is with arithmetic calculations.

The prices I'm working on are as follows (prices not to win in brackets):

4/6 Manchester United (11/10)
1/2 Liverpool (6/4)
4/9 Arsenal (13/8)
4/6 Chelsea (11/10)

If you can evaluate how the prices have been formed, you have passed the exam on how to become an odds compiler. The prices for all four teams (and none of them) to win should be easy to evaluate with a simple accumulator. Simply multiply the prices for the four teams which equates to 5/1. The offer of 11/2 is there to encourage punters to play all four teams. Use the same accumulator for the teams NOT to win, which produces odds of 28/1, which we promote to 33/1. That's the easy part over with for now. How do we find the correct price for one winning team, two and three winners from the favourites?

The secret lies within the not to win scenario. The prices for teams NOT to win in all of the following scenarios will be shown in brackets. Taking the one winner situation initially, you have four accumulators to determine. The way to determine one winner is to create accumulators for one of the four teams to win, the odds for which are multiplied by the prices for the other three teams NOT to win.

Manchester United: 4/6 x (6/4) x (13/8) x (11/10) = 22/1
Liverpool: 1/2 x (11/10) x 13/8) x (11/10) = 16/1
Arsenal: 4/9 x (11/10) x (6/4) x (11/10) = 16/1
Chelsea: 4/6: x (11/10) x (6/4) x (13/8) = 22/1

The next job is to determine the collective percentages of those four equations, which equal 20.2%.

As a punter, you should already know that there are six doubles in four matches, the same as yankees etc in the horse racing sector, so it follows that there are six accumulators to deduce to find the price for two winners from the four football teams.

Manchester United – 4/6 & Liverpool – 1/2 x (13/8) x (11/10) = 12/1
Manchester United – 4/6 & Arsenal – 4/9 x (6/4) x (11/10) = 16/1
Manchester United – 4/6 & Chelsea – 4/6 x (6/4) x (13/8) = 18/1
Liverpool – 1/2 & Arsenal – 4/9 x (11/10) & (11/10) = 17/2

Liverpool – 1/2 & Chelsea – 4/6 x (13/8) & 11/10 = 12/1
Arsenal – 4/9 & Chelsea – 4/6 x (11/10) & 6/4 = 12/1

The percentages for these prices accumulates to 44.8%.
The number of trebles in four selections is four:

Manchester United – 4/6, Liverpool – 1/2 &
     Arsenal – 4/9 x (11/10) = 13/2
Manchester United – 4/6, Liverpool – 1/2 &
     Chelsea – 4/6 x (13/8) = 10/1
Manchester United – 4/6, Arsenal – 4/9 &
     Chelsea – 4/6 x (6/4) = 9/1
Liverpool – 1/2, Arsenal – 4/9 &
     Chelsea – 4/6 x (11/10) = 13/2

The prices for these trebles accumulate to 45.7%.

Where do we go from here? First determine the percentages
you are willing to bet to, whereby my prices of 13/8 – 13/8
– 5/1 – 11/2 – 33/1 accumulate to 111.3%. Bearing in mind
that you cannot change the prices of all four selections
(and none) winning, you now have to determine the prices
of the 1-2-3 scenarios. Add together the percentages of
the no winners (33/1) and all four successful teams (11/2),
which equates to 18.4%. You must now deduct that 18.4
figure from your required TOTAL percentage (111.3) which
means that you have 92.9% to work with.

The percentages for the 1-2-3 winners scenarios (20.2 –
44.8 – 45.7) totals 110.7%. The final mathematical work to
be completed, is to divide the 92.9 by 110.7 which equates
to 0.839. You have basically reduced the percentages
mathematically, to enable the results to join the 11/2 and
33/1 prices to form your book. The one winner scenario is

evaluated by multiplying the original collective percentage of 20.2% x .839 = 16.9 (5/1 nearest price). Two winners (same principle): 44.8 x .839 = 37.6 (13/8 nearest price). Three winners: 45.7 x .839 = 38.3 (13/8 nearest price). Which completes the book of:

   33/1 no winners
   5/1 one winner
   13/8 two winners
   13/8 three winners
   11/2 all four winners

Utilising the professional approach, ask yourself if you are happy with the prices you are offering. By offering these prices, I am suggesting that there is marginally more chance of one winner occurring compared to all four. Equally the coupled prices equate to:

   4/1: None or one winner
   5/6: One or two winners
   3/10: Two or three winners
   10/11: Three or all four winners
   8/11: 0-1-2 winners
   1/14: 1-2-3 winners
   1/11: 2-3-4 winners

I am happy to offer those prices given the initial odds (4/6 –1/2 – 4/9 – 4/6) for each team to win. And you thought compiling odds was a piece of cake!

This betting scenario can (of course) relate to favourites, nominated horses, players, sides in horse racing, tennis rubbers or cricket teams.

CHAPTER 12

Summing Up

If you have managed to read through all the chapters in this publication, you will realise why a bookmaker's correct title is turf accountant, with the emphasis very much on accountant!

The Art of Bookmaking is about being lucky of course. A bookmaker must also be greedy in his approach to business (but not on the exchanges), accommodating, inventive, brave and perhaps above all other things, accurate and consistent. Which stance did you take on the 'Harchibald' argument in chapter one?

The correct stance would have been to decide what was right from your viewpoint. Irrespective of whether you agreed with the journalist or my argument, you should have made a decision from your perspective and, in hindsight, the right view might have been somewhere in between our two different standpoints. My basic argument was that Harchibald should not be offered at a price where punters could secure a bet to nothing, especially with a bridle horse who always looked a champion until he saw the wining post. The journalist (possibly taking the poor record of 'Bula' winners into account) didn't fancy the horse to go one better in the Champion Hurdle in 2006, having finished as an unlucky loser the previous year. The stance to take might be the one that suggests that I was right from an each way perspective, whilst the journalist had a point that Harchibald should not have been promoted to favourite on the strength of one victory over mediocre opposition. The best option therefore, is to possibly offer a win only price about Noel Meade's raider, whereby you accommodate punters who fancy the horse at 5/1 (as an example) but not the sharks who view the place terms as icing on the potential cake.

The same situation arises with football betting on the Premiership on a year by year basis. Bookmakers price up the Premiership knowing that only a few teams can win the title, yet they are duty bound to cover their backs from a place perspective. Tottenham might be the best example in recent years, because the White Hart Lane outfit has flattered to deceive so many times, yet equally, there has always been that sneaking suspicion that the North London side could scrape into third place in a bad year.

Tottenham have therefore been quoted at 50/1 at times, even though their true price of actually lifting the Premiership trophy has been 500/1 as long as I can remember. With Chelsea already long odds on to win the 2006/2007 title, there could be plenty of value to be had as a bookmaker/layer in offering the other 19 Premiership teams at inflated prices but not in an each way market. A place only book might be one to open, taking Chelsea out of the equation perhaps.

In all of these circumstances, I am suggesting that *The Art of Bookmaking* is creating novelty books, based on simple mathematics, which is the way odds must always be presented.

A bookmaker/layer must also scrutinise what is on offer with other companies and change the scenario around to their preference. Whilst I have attempted to manufacture new markets with examples in this publication, there is a strong argument to keep things simple, preferably utilising betting scenarios which are already in place and tweaking them into attracting new clients with variations that you (the bookmaker) have created.

The Art of Bookmaking is to increase potential percentages as well as the turnover, with inventive betting opportunities. A final example of the point I am trying to make, relates to what will be the opening games of the new football season in August 2006.

Are you, as a bookmaker, going to let the frenzy of the World Cup die away after the final is played in July?

There is invariably additional interest to a new season after the World Cup Finals have been contested, so why not take advantage of the scenario? As a possible example, take five popular teams (outside of Chelsea in this instance) and invent a book that relates to the first three games for each team in the opening few weeks of the season. Use these examples as a potential market:

Arsenal play: Bolton (A) – Man City (H) – Fulham (A)
Liverpool play: Newcastle (H) – Man Utd (A) –
    Bolton (H)
Man Utd play: Chelsea (H) – Newcastle (A) –
    Wigan (H)
Tottenham play: Fulham (H) – Wigan (A) –
    Liverpool (H)
Newcastle play: Liverpool (A) – Man Utd (H) –
    Blackburn (A)

The market is based on which team will amass the most points, with goal difference determining the outcome in the event of a draw. If two teams are still tied given that scenario, you might decide to keep both parties happy by calling a dead heat, though whatever situation you prefer to advertise, you must make the rules and conditions clear, as in all marketing exercises.

I'm going to leave the actual odds compiling to you but you should note that some of the teams competing in this betting scenario are playing each other, which will have a direct bearing on the outcome, in all probability. What I am not leaving to you however, is the potential advertising of such a bet, because this is another area where current, independent, bookmakers let themselves down, in my humble opinion. You have to speculate to accumulate as the saying goes in the world of gambling but yet again, we find bookmakers waiting for the public to come to them, rather than the reverse.

The World Cup finishes a few weeks before the schools break up for the summer holidays (in England and Wales at least), when most people take their summer vacations. With hundreds of thousands of potential football supporters and punters heading for the likes of Blackpool and Torquay, without mentioning all the holiday parks the length and breadth of the country, bookmakers miss the opportunity of hitting the public when the holidaymakers have time to concentrate of what is on offer for a new season.

With Chelsea dominating the markets just now, this is the perfect opportunity of advertising a new slant on the football front, as punters look for an alternative betting scenario, given that the London team seemingly has the Premiership in the bag before a ball is kicked. What's wrong with printing flyers given the example I offered and distributing the odds en masse throughout the land? Contact guest houses, holiday parks and hotels and knock up a deal whereby your coupons can be distributed to all the holidaymakers through the vacation season. New clients will emerge because they have been attracted by the wager that you have to offer and there is every chance that these punters will become regular callers from that day forward.

Use whatever example you offer to best advantage, whereby the percentage you use when totalling up the odds is attractive to the punter, yet is safe for you to advertise. If you adopt a bet with five possible outcomes as in the example, you might look to an over round book of 12.9%, which should suit everyone.

You will note that I have utilised two teams from the capital and one each from Manchester, Liverpool and Newcastle. The Art of Bookmaking is to sell your product to as many potential clients as you can and London, Manchester, Liverpool and Newcastle will do nicely for starters. You don't have to limit the scenario to the UK of course. The marketing people amongst you will already have thought of overseas travellers, whereby airports, service stations and coach companies could be contacted. Never put limits on your potential client base.

From an independent boomaker's perspective, you should always ensure that whatever bet you accommodate is paid up front. The days of slates are over. Not only does a bookmaker lose money when a punter is allowed to run up debts... the layer also loses the client's business.

CHAPTER 13

2006/2007 Events Update

The best advantage a punter can secure, is if they take a stance against a bookmaker who has taken a stand on any given event, which is why I am going to start this final chapter updating the following sport.

Golf – The Ryder Cup
(Straffan, Co. Kildare – 22-24 September):

At the time of writing, one or two bookmakers have gone out on a limb looking to lay the United States for the 2006 competition.

Ladbrokes (for betting shop punters) and Skybet and Sporting Odds (for Internet players) all offer 11/8 for the Americans to lift the trophy and whether you fancy the Yankees to strike gold or not, only the most churlish of punters would argue against the fact that 11/8 (42%) appears to be a generous quote. Taking the price now will give punters a strong foothold in the competition, because there is a good possibility that the prices of the other two options will drift in places from their current best quotes, which are as follows:

Europe: Evens (Paddy Power)
The Draw: 10/1 (Betfred) and 11/1 on the exchanges.

The best prices add up to just 100.4% and the advice is to play the United States at 11/8 and wait for the other prices to drift to take advantage of an over broke book by the collective layers. I am mindful that the European players will receive frenzied support from the local Irish fans, whilst Ian Woosnam has secured the right to make the fairways and greens with a European bias with the links style of pitch and run play. As suggested earlier in this publication, the prices will vary considerably over the three days but 11/8 (USA) will create a positive start to your ledger.

It is the Americans who tend to land the big victories during the course of the year and if Tiger and his playmates dominate the week by week headlines, I could envisage the price of the Europeans drifting quite early in the season, especially if the USA players run riot in The Masters at Augusta.

The layers are looking to 'get' the US money into their satchels convinced that 'team spirit' will overcome any deficiency that the European team might take into the match, but this is a dangerous stance to adopt. The scenario has worked in favour of the Europeans before, but it should be remembered that such psychology takes on a new perspective when the original outsiders have now become the favourites to win the event. The underdogs have fought tenaciously as teams down the years in almost every sport you can name. How else could Wimbledon have beaten Liverpool in the F.A. Cup Final in 1988, when man for man they were facing a hopeless task?

Would Wimbledon have had so much blood coursing

through their veins if the bookmakers had priced them up as favourites for the game? Take that thought with you when you consider betting on the Ryder Cup this autumn.

Football – The 2006/07 Premiership season.

Football is becoming an increasingly 'mental' sport, especially at the top level, where psychology is as important as the talent of the players that take to the field. The first goal of a match dictates the rest of the game, yet 'Sven' (to name but one) does not seem prepared to accept the situation. If I asked you to name the top player in the Premiership in the season just finished, players such as Lampard, Terry and Gerrard would probably spring to mind. What you and 'Sven' should take into account however, is that only one player in the top flight of domestic football scored the first goal of the game eight times last season, and his name is Darren Bent. Indeed, Charlton only scored the opening goal of the game on twelve occasions from thirty-eight opportunities, yet Bent scored eight of those important goals!

This is the type of crucial information that you should digest before calculating odds, whether you intend to be a layer or a player. The Art of Bookmaking (as the forward suggests) is written in a manner which leaves the emphasis on you the reader, to determine how you want to develop your greater understanding of compiling odds. You might consider that Beattie (Everton) remains an underrated player (another forward that Sven turned down), especially as the old fashioned centre forward scored the opening goal of the game on seven occasions during the 2005/2006 season. Further investigation would lead you to deduce however, that all seven of Beattie's opening goals were scored at Goodison Park; hence as a potential bookmaker, you should restrict the odds when Everton are entertaining the opposition, but 'lay' the forward away from home.

Goal scoring is about confidence as much as anything else, and some forwards struggle to match their home performances on their travels. This is not the case with Tottenham's Robbie Keane however, as the Irish international opened the scoring on five occasions away from White Hart Lane last year. Whatever big name that Tottenham might sign in the month or years to come will struggle to match Keane from a mental perspective, and that is what makes Robbie such an important and valuable asset.

How many times did you (as a punter) back a Premiership match to end in a draw last season? Unless you secured a usually unavailable price of 4/1 or more, you were wasting your money in general terms. Just twenty per cent of the Premiership games ended all square last season, and as a 'bookmaker' you should seek to turn these facts to your advantage.

You can still lay the draw in these games on the exchanges at 5/2 and 11/4, as punters accept that an average price of just 12/5 is available in the betting outlets. By laying the draw you are finding an edge against your fellow trader, and fundamentally, this must be your aim for this coming season.

With just three results to consider, some potential bookmakers will feel uneasy about laying a seemingly exaggerated price about the stalemate, but such people should study the facts and steam in, because that's what bookmaking is (or should be) all about. Armed with the facts and stats that you have read in this book, you now need the 'balls' to back up the information because the bookmaking business is not all about money and knowledge. Unless you have the courage of your conviction, you will go where so many bookies have gone in the past.

John McCririck is a lot of things but he is no fool. As a failed bookmaker (and I know the feeling), John will tell you that there are 2000 less independent bookmakers now compared to the old days. So many more shops would have closed down in the last few years but for the gaming machines that can be found in the licensed premises these days, and betting shop bookmakers are not so much 'layers' these days but agents who cream off their expenses from 'punters' who rarely bet on horse racing.

Independent bookmakers are fast becoming punters themselves, looking to beat their fellow punters on the exchanges in much the same way that I have played the toteplacepot down the years.

If you play the exchanges either as a layer or a player, you are seeking to beat your fellow 'punter', pure and simple. It is a scenario that I have adopted with the toteplacepot and fellow punters are so much easier to defeat than established bookmakers.

When you take stock of what you have read in this publication, the one thing you should do is to dwell on the information you have gleaned. Do not make a snap decision on whether you want to become the next 'new bookie' on the block, or give up your 'day job' thinking that you now have what it takes to change direction in life. Digest the facts, make observations and treat each new morning as a learning day, which I am still doing after thirty five years in the business.

'Play' at becoming a bookmaker if you like, by laying and striking imaginary bets and enter the results down in debit and credit columns. Do not withdraw large sums of money and start waging war with layers and players until you have a definite strategy. Only then should you decide if you are ready to take the 'Art of Bookmaking' a stage further.